No BS!

The Art of Agency

BRAD ALLEN

Published in Ireland 2025.

Published by TPAssist LIMITED.

ISBN 978-1-0686295-7-0

TPAssist LIMITED
14 Penrose Wharf
Cork, T23 W040, Ireland

www.tpassist.com

Dedication

To those I treasure, who've help me see how to live
beyond the script.

Contents

INTRODUCTION

Chapter 1: Ditching the default

The simulation has ended; welcome to reality.

Certainty

You may be having fun, making progress, achieving things, but still be left with a sense that something is missing. You will probably have questions, even when everything seems to be going okay. You may want to know if you are doing enough to be a good spouse, parent, son/daughter, sibling, friend, co-worker, employee, and manager. You may want to know if you are doing enough so that you won't be alone. You may want to know if what you are doing would ensure that you will have enough money to have a decent living and provide for those you love. You may want to know if you are doing enough to take care of yourself, so you don't drop dead well before your time.

Allow these questions to fester too long and you will likely search for certainty. Certainty that you are forging the right path. Certainty that every choice you make is the right choice to make at that time.

Without the right skills, the search for certainty will become a burden. The burden of your choices. Without a crystal ball to see the future, and without the right skills, relief from the burden of choice means giving up your ability to choose. Once you stop making choices or, more importantly, once you stop taking responsibility for the outcomes, you will be freed, and relieved of the burden of choice. But that is only the beginning of your real problems.

Surrendering

There are many who have seen success financially, have held power, have been super-fit, or devoted rafts of time to charities, but have then settled for something less when it comes to 'being'. They choose to hide behind those aspects of their lives where they are succeeding. They choose to self-censor. They choose to comply with bogus rules and regulations. They strive to do things that go against common sense.

Life is challenging. You may be confronted by things that don't go the way you had hoped. When that happens, you face a choice: look for new ways to progress or surrender.

Surrendering is things like disengagement, overeating, inactivity, binge-watching and excessive gaming. Surrendering underlies self-censoring, compliance with nonsense rules and regulations and going against common sense. Surrendering also has more committed forms, like alcohol, drugs, working long hours, and even fitness related activities at the expense of everything else. Surrendering also applies to selling yourself short, i.e., perhaps accepting a promotion or new job that isn't really for you. Perhaps it pays well or has other benefits. But goes against your principles, or was offered to you for the wrong reasons, i.e., as a favour or to meet identity quotas.

Surrendering is also where you waste your time and energy. Where you don't care enough about being the best you can be. You keep busy, bank the pay-check, and then collect things to help maintain the comfort. You avoid confronting the things that will really bring meaning. You fear making any real changes, and letting go of some of the comforts. You fear what you would have to face if you couldn't hide behind the comforting but limiting beliefs you have about yourself (i.e., you hide behind the beliefs that no longer serve you).

Avoidance of responsibility

Avoidance of responsibility comes in several forms. It can make an appearance when you see others or other things as holding you back or the cause of the dramas that surround you. It can occur when someone does something to upset you, withhold something or get in your way. It can show up when you perceive yourself as a victim, regardless of the actual circumstances. It is present when you see the only path forward as being for another person to change or someone else to intervene in the situation. It is there when your mind is closed to other possibilities or ways of doing something.

In all forms of avoidance of responsibility, in effect, you are giving someone else the responsibility of resolving your situation. When you do that, you give up your autonomy. You give over to the mercy of someone else's will. You are at risk of having to feel, think and act in a manner that serves their best interests, not yours. You also can open yourself up to being abused or taken advantage of. While the behaviours of others might have you feeling small, useless and unimportant, giving into it is avoiding responsibility.

The Absence

Obsession with certainty, surrendering, or avoiding responsibility, have one important thing in common. When there, you don't think for yourself. You are under the influence of the desires and wants of others. You risk being manipulated by individuals or entities that behave dishonestly or maliciously.

The Antidote

The antidote to an obsession with certainty, surrendering, or avoiding responsibility, is agency.

Agency is the process of using your own truth to create wonderful, productive, and engaging experiences for you and others.

Unfortunately, agency isn't easy. There are two opposing forces at play. There is a trade-off you must engage with. On one hand, you want to be yourself and aligned with your own purpose and identity. On the other hand, by your nature, you want to be social and be part of something. That requires you to compromise and be part of someone else's purpose and identity. However, if you try too hard to be part of someone else's reality, you risk being what others want you to be. Moreover, if you say and do exactly what you feel is right for you at every moment, you will inevitably offend someone else. That limits your ability to be social and benefit from what others can offer you. While if you constantly filter what you say and do, you corrupt your responses, and that impacts your ability to experience the world as you may want to experience it.

Agency, more specifically, the agency trade-off, therefore, is a balancing act of satisfying your own needs and the needs of others.

Agency is also something else. Agency is when there is close to no resistance in your mind to what you say, do, and experience. It is when you get what you want without compromising yourself or others. It is when the burdens you carry feel almost weightless.

When you do or experience something in the present moment, that honours your current self but has detrimental consequences for your future self, you are creating unnecessary resistance. A simplistic example would be eating a lot of chocolate cake. It has engagement in the present moment, however if you don't make use of the excess sugars, you are creating problems for your future self in the form of unnecessary weight gain.

When you do or experience something in the present moment, that both honours your current self and has only positive consequences for your future self, you reduce the resistance. For example, when you just have one piece of chocolate cake, which is proportionate to what you have recently eaten and your immediate plans to make use of the sugars, you don't create further problems for your future self.

Agency isn't about trying to eliminate resistance completely; it's the resistance and uncertainty that gives us the power of choice. Through choosing, we embark on an adventure. This adventure, or more precisely, the act of taking responsibility for our choices, becomes a profound source of meaning. The key is to recognize resistance and manage it effectively. You need to become much more comfortable with being uncomfortable. Once you achieve this, you've found the antidote. This is agency. And this is precisely what this book explores, without the usual B.S.

How to use this book

This book features twenty-seven self-coaching topics, each neatly organized under the heading 'Coaching Corner'. These topics are enriched with insights on behaviour and personal experiences, divided into four distinct parts.

Part 1 explores how limiting beliefs—those that no longer serve you—and their associated behaviours can let you down, especially when interacting with others. Part 2 delves into realistic optimism, examining how it provides a solid platform for making choices. Part 3 covers thinking, emotions, socializing, and the physical aspects of agency. The final part of the book examines what helps create momentum, leveraging the ideas introduced in Parts 1 through 3.

To make the most of this book, consider reading it from start to finish, then revisiting specific self-coaching topics as needed. Alternatively, feel free to jump directly to any topic that catches your interest to explore its immediate relevance to you. You can find all the 'Coaching Corner' topics at bradallen.coach.

Coaching Corner Topics

PART 1:
BE TRUE TO YOURSELF

Chapter 2: Navigate

Agency, or the lack of it, shows up in many places.

Permission

Aligning with the desires of others, is not a bad thing, so long as you understand the reasons and choose it for yourself. In aligning with others, you are giving up some degree of decision making. You are in effect giving others permission to make some of your decisions for you. The risk here is that giving permission can enable further liberties to be taken. Before you know it, your choices are being taken away without any negotiation. And this is where the damage can be done. This is where you will find it hard to be true to yourself and act with agency.

It can break your flow, when someone takes your choices away. When someone does something in your name it must be something that aligns with what you want. It is even harder when that action is done with a smile and is in a context where confrontation causes further stress. When done well, the behaviour has all the indications of genuine concern. When it isn't. It's just being manipulative or needy, and it is simply bullying.

Bullying takes many forms. Someone going behind your back and using lies or half-truths to manipulate situations to suit their own needs is one form. However, the behaviour can be just as effective in plain sight if the perpetrator has enough skills to hide their intentions.

The deeper and more disturbing form of bullying comes when it's hard to discern if someone is really trying to help or if they are being manipulative. Passive-aggressive behaviour, indirect manipulation and resistance, has a public form. Acting in plain sight of others creates a smoke screen that hides the truth. The action may be hurtful, or it may involve giving a compliment or advice that appears to be constructive and, in your interest, when it is really something you don't agree with.

An example might be when a manager tells the team that 'Mal wants help finishing the sales pitch', when Mal knows the manager simply doesn't agree with the direction Mal is taking. The manager wants to appear empathetic and empowering, not controlling and interfering. If Mal speaks up and contradicts the manager, Mal will look petty, and silly. Another example might be when a spouse disagrees with their significant other about the use of lights in the house. At a dinner party they might casually say something like 'Kim loves the brightness and turns lights on all over the house'. And one final example might be when a committee member is annoyed with another member for not agreeing to help lobby a change in the time of a meeting. The annoyed member might say in front of Val and the group, 'Val is very busy, juggling lots of really important work'. It is hard for others to know what's really going on, unless they have deep knowledge of the background and relationship of the bully and person being bullied.

The impact on your enjoyment and experience can be severely compromised when you aren't able to effectively handle this abusive behaviour. When you continue to give up your agency and give permission for your choices to be made by someone else, you risk becoming alienated and marginalized.

The artist

It is one thing to allow someone to blatantly reduce your choices: it's another thing altogether to invite it.

Even with experience, it is still possible to fall prey to passive manipulative behaviours. This is especially true of those you might naively look up to. Perhaps you admire their calmness and appearance of all knowing and intelligence. Perhaps you adopt some of their ways of working. That may be okay for a time. However, if they aren't what they appear, you may start to notice things being a little off. If your admiration is strong, you may even do your best to manage things around them or cover for them. At some point you might even try to alert them of a problem. If they are the passive manipulative type, things won't go well for you when you do. They will likely use your 'feedback' against you. They may make it look like you were the cause of the problem. They even may do that in front of others to protect themselves. This isn't good for you. The artist won't think twice about throwing you under the bus if it serves their purposes.

The helpful

Even harder still is when the manipulation is subtle. It makes it harder to detect and avoid. We all have experienced someone who is always doing 'helpful' things for others without being asked. They are usually the first ones to pop over with a tray of lasagne when someone is sick or there is a bereavement.

Without you soliciting their assistance they'll buy things you don't need or do things 'for you', but rarely in a way that helps you. As they are doing all of those 'helpful' deeds, they expect accolades at the time and then use sweetness to bully their way into favours later. Just before asking for your help, they'll ask you about that book they got you last month. They go out of their way to be interested in things you are doing so they can use it to their advantage. For example, they will take a keen interest in your commitments. Then, when you indicate a gap in your schedule, they'll suddenly have an idea. Usually it is something they need, and it will, astonishingly, fit precisely into your schedule gap. You get stuck with no way out. They already know you can't turn them down because they know you don't have any commitments at that time. While they will suggest otherwise, all of this will be in their best interest, not yours. They will be reluctant to ask openly for your help, because they want to avoid any sense that they owe you. They want to stay in control. They will go to efforts so that it looks like they are doing you a favour by giving you something worthwhile to fill your spare time. They do this to make it look like whatever it is, it's for your benefit not theirs. Then if you do find something that you need their help with, they will make all kinds of seemingly legitimate excuses and then over-enthusiastically promise to help 'next time', which never happens. Clearly this does not apply to everyone that turns up with a tray of lasagne or does things we didn't ask for. Thankfully, many acts like these are done with an honest interest in giving and expecting nothing in return.

Assuming the best of others

From time to time, you will come across a bad actor, an individual or entity that behaves dishonestly, maliciously, or in ways that are contrary to the interests of others or societal norms. The word 'actor' is used in the label because these types of people appear something that they are not. Their manner is good and wholesome, and their behaviour appears to be in your interest. When in truth, they are only doing what they are doing to take advantage of you. Bad actors could be thought of as having one or more of the Dark Triad traits. These include narcissism, Machiavellianism and psychopathy. Furthermore, some will draw on the Dark Tetrad, which is the Dark Triad, plus Sadism.

Fortunately, most of the people who get in your way or make life less than ideal for you, won't be bad actors. They may just be using behaviours which aren't in your interest. Often it is a case of someone following, without question, a path and set of behaviours defined by someone else. This is the basis of a 'borrowed belief'. More on that later.

At all times you simply need to look for what does not feel right and look for what is important to you. You need to distance yourself from those who try to compromise your choices, without your permission. You need to get better skills to confront those that you must endure. You must find the space needed to stay true to what you value.

Chapter 3: Invest

Agency is not just a solo act.

Holding back

Relationships start at the first moment we meet someone, be it in person or via an electronic exchange. The quality of the relationship can be built over short or prolonged periods. The same relationship can give us the most amazing experience, as well as the most dreadful. It is not clear what always works and what always fails.

When you engage in an interaction with someone new, the quality and outcomes will depend on your state of mind. If you are fearful and judgmental, you are likely to experience something that leaves you frustrated, blaming, and underwhelmed. If you are willing to share, ask, and be asked, the difficult questions, you are more likely to experience something real and rich.

When you hold back, you compromise the potential. This comes in many forms, like holding back what you think or believe is important, as we explored in chapter two. Another form would be presenting a version of yourself that is not you; but is what you think the other person wants to see and experience. We will explore this further in chapter four. A further form would be second-guessing what the other person wants before you share, rather than just sharing or asking them. A simple example of this would be agreeing to have a glass of wine when you really want a peppermint tea. All these forms of holding back are defence mechanisms based on fear of ridicule, rejection and getting hurt. They hide your true desires, wants and needs. Holding back protects you but blocks you from learning and growing. However, if you are comfortable sharing and learning about what you can do better, you open the door to connection.

The yacht

Solid and lasting relationships require effort.

Consider thinking of the process of starting a relationship, being like buying a yacht together. For the yacht to be reliable it needs to be maintained. The same is true of productive and long-lasting relationships.

When you take delivery of your new shiny yacht, you might ease yourselves into it slowly. You might take it out and about in relatively calm waters. You will test it somewhat and get used to making it move well. You will have some fun, just you two, enjoying this new thing. You won't be on the yacht all the time. You will park it back in the marina and go off and do your own things at times. Then at other times, you won't be alone (i.e., you might sail with others in a flotilla of yachts).

Like all new things, new yachts don't need much maintenance at the start. You simply get into it, drive on, and have fun. However, over time things break. Perhaps it might be pushed a little too hard or run too close to something. Then after a while, perhaps there is a need for a new coat of paint/varnish or some repairs to the woodwork. Perhaps the sails and engine need repairing or servicing. Further down the line, the yacht might need to be taken out of the water and given some major repairs to strengthen the superstructure to support more (i.e., a larger team or new family members). This also might be necessary so that the yacht performs well in more difficult waters (e.g., economic downturns, ill-health, or other changed circumstances).

Even when new things come with user manuals, who reads them? It's more likely that getting to know your yacht is based on trial and error, and perhaps some training if you are a little organized and forward thinking. Learning to make the most of the yacht is relatively easy, in that it is something that has immediate and more tangible benefits. Mastering the art of maintaining the yacht might be a little harder for most, simply because, it is harder to apply the discipline to learning and doing something when the benefits are only realized down the track. Furthermore, since this is a shared endeavour, your ability to effectively and efficiently work together will be highly dependent on what you know about your own abilities. If you only have an inkling of what each can bring to the table, you might waste energy trying to do something that someone else can already do better. This learning, or appreciation of who you are, will have a direct impact on how much you get out of the new thing. This appreciation of who you are will also impact how well you do the more difficult job of maintenance.

When you sail into troubled waters, the lack of maintenance becomes more evident (i.e., if the hull leaks or the hatches and windows don't close properly). When this happens, you run the risk of sinking. Equally, if the engine doesn't work well or the sails are torn or worn out, they won't push the yacht at the speed needed to successfully get through the storm. And finally, if you haven't fully explored and developed your understanding of what abilities each has, you may lose your heads or fail to take the actions needed to weather the storm.

Sailing successfully through any weather, be it calm or rough, is down to preparation. The more you know about the capabilities of the yacht and yourselves, the higher the probability that you will get where you want to be and have a great time as you do it. Preparation is both learning and maintenance. Yacht-ownership-related learning is about understanding the physical elements and using physical tools. Relationship-related learning is about knowing what you value and what your individual traits are. The best way to build that understanding is to be open and honest with each other.

Sparks cause fires

Cracks in relationships become more prevalent and are harder to fix when there is insufficient investment and preparation. Relationships are often talked about as starting with a 'spark' but over time, having lost their 'fire'. Let's look at fires for a moment, specifically bushfires. Forest and bushfires are a major problem in many parts of the world. The dry and hot climate is a very fertile place for rampant and uncontrollable bushfires that put property and lives at risk. At times during the year, no open fires are allowed. During the cooler and wetter times of the year, great efforts are made to clear firebreaks, keep grass low, and back-burn tracks of land. All this preparation is to help prevent and manage fires during the dry season.

The threat of fire comes from all corners. Some are started through neglect and failure to adhere to the fire ban. Some are purposely lit by disturbed individuals. Others are caused naturally, e.g., through lightning strikes. While potentially catastrophic, fires aren't all bad. In fact, many of the indigenous trees and plants have become so accustomed to the fires that they have evolved ways to regrow. Some ecosystems totally rely on the fires to prevent overgrowth and thus create the right conditions for survival. These ecosystems can rebuild themselves from the ashes and thrive. The damage caused by the fire makes the whole system stronger. This is the same with relationships. Conflict under the right conditions and with the right preparation can make the relationship stronger. However, conflict in the ill-prepared relationship can be terminal.

Things get harder in relationships as you take on more complexity, e.g., children, aging parents, the aging process, or less than perfect careers.

If you don't work hard to keep on top of things, the relationship struggles and eventually breaks.

The three Cs

To succeed, intimate relationships must involve attention to the three Cs: chemistry, cognitive alignment, and context. Without attention to these three aspects, relationships will falter and drain both party's energy.

Chemistry is obvious, but often neglected. For it to work, both must truly lust for each other. That doesn't always happen. Perhaps there is a degree of desperation, perhaps there is something about the intimacy that is new and exciting, perhaps their ego is telling them they will look good together. Unfortunately, a compromise here will be fatal later. While perhaps neglected, chemistry is the easiest to get right. The test is simple. One simply needs to ask if they are totally attracted to this person when they are at their worst, physically? That lust must be there when they meet at the end of an exhausting day, stressed and preoccupied. If that happens the chemistry is solid. If they are only physically attracted to them when they are at their best, things aren't how they should be. It's true that over time one might get a little too comfortable and take less care of oneself than one should. Nevertheless, even as one grows old, becomes less firm, gains or loses hair and gets a little more rounded, the core of the beauty will remain and that's what creates the chemistry. Without the chemistry they are just pretending.

Cognitive alignment is crucial for longevity, but not so important in casual relationships. Cognitive alignment includes aspects of personality and how we interact with the world. For longevity, couples need to have alignment in sense of humour, similar levels of emotional intelligence, similar core values, some similar interests, and a degree of alignment of ideologies and other life philosophies. Sense of humour is the most important of all these aspects and is likely to be aligned from the start. This is, of course, if one is being honest and not just letting primal urges drive laughter even when they don't get the other person's humour. Life is hard but it will become unbearable if one is not sharing laughter at oneself and the world. A similar level of emotional intelligence is important, so they relate properly. Emotional intelligence is something one grows. It's not fixed, but relationships must start at a similar level. This is so that one isn't having to educate or bring the other person along. Having a teacher-and-student dynamic can be fun in aspects of a relationship, but it gets tiresome if it's one-sided all the time. Being the basis of decisions, and beliefs and behaviours, core values will shape who one is and how one grows. A big gap here will get in the way of the relationship developing properly. Similar interests create opportunities for shared experiences. It's during those shared experiences that laughter is found, and learning takes place. Finally, having some degree of alignment in ideologies and other life philosophies ensures violence doesn't break out on the first encounter. Alignment here ensures couples have things to share that they are passionate about, but not so different that they simply have nothing to engage on together.

Context is the reality that exists at the start of a relationship. This will include habits and routines, physical condition, mental condition, commitments to others, financial flexibility, baggage, and skills in managing complexity. There is always context, no matter the stage of life. This context will both enable and get in the way of a strong and lasting relationship. Lack of flexibility in many of these aspects will prevent meeting the right person. When a meeting does take place, inflexibility makes it harder to experience each other fully. It just isn't realistic that one will be able to keep everything the same after they meet someone. They must make changes. They might need to spend less time with those they care about, to make room for the new person. They might need to change some of their routines and habits to fit better with the other's availability. They might need to invite them into their existing activities and share them with them. They might need to work on their physical condition so that they can have better sex. They might need to seek help to remove more of the baggage. They might need to reduce their financial security somewhat, so that they have the means to engage fully in new and shared experiences. An unwillingness to share and integrate new people into existing routines, experiences, and friendships keeps others out.

Of the three Cs, while all are necessary, cognitive alignment is the most important. Having the ability to connect with each other on similar emotional and intellectual levels enables us to learn about each other's needs, our individual contexts, and is required to create the new and shared conditions necessary for rich and lasting relationships.

The potential of the union

While healthy intimate relations are very important, this chapter is about more than that. It is about how you approach relationships of any kind. When you put your perceptions in between you and others, you limit the potential for rich and rewarding cognitive and physical unions. When you are not authentic in relationships, the trust is harder to build. The secrets you hold on to, keep you from reaching your potential. When you are allowing your authentic self to shine through, your relationships grow and thrive.

Chapter 4: Take down the sign

Agency can be a tricky character.

The Greengrocer's Dilemma

Milan Kundera's 1984 novel, The Unbearable Lightness of Being, set in 1968 communist Prague, includes the story of a greengrocer putting up a sign in his window that reads 'Workers of the world, unite!'. He put the sign up, not because he believed in Marxism, but because if he didn't hang that sign, he and his family might suffer at the hands of the communists. By putting up the sign he was participating in the collective act of self-deception. He was supporting the collective lie that many undertook to protect themselves from persecution at the hands of brainwashed adherents, ideologues and corrupt opportunists.

It is true that the greengrocer's choice paved an easier path for him and his family, for the time being. The act of compliance, however, had significant implications. As Hannah Arendt in her many writings illustrates, this scenario can be seen as a demonstration of how ordinary people can become complicit in oppressive systems through small, seemingly innocuous acts of compliance.

In going with the norms, complying with what is asked of us or choosing to self-censor, we must be certain that we are doing it for the right reasons. Yes, we must act in our own interest and the interests of those dear to us, but we can't lose sight of how our actions may adversely affect our future options.

Status and brands

Status has a role to play in how we balance our needs and the needs of the groups we want to be part of. A large part of status is the brands we have on display, be it our clothing, the car or even the suburb we live in. As with all aspects of the agency trade-off, the brands on display mustn't become who we are.

The personality test

Personality tests, like a 'Big Five' traits-based tests or the Myers-Briggs Type Indicator (MBTI), have a place but they need to be considered with caution. Unfortunately, if the test is poorly administered you might adopt a belief that you are one way or another, when that might not be the case. You may even start adjusting your behaviours and habits to 'fit' with the statements shared in the test results.

Personality tests are self-reported and as such, they are relative to how you are feeling and what is going on around you when you take the test. Furthermore, while these tests do their best to catch attempts to mislead the results by asking the same question in several different ways, with practice and good knowledge of how the test works, the test taker can sway the results in the direction they want. This isn't helpful for recruiters using the tests as part of employee placement. Nor is it useful if you want to really understand more about yourself. All of this has the potential to hold you back and reduce your agency.

In Part 3, we will explore better ways to build understanding of who you are.

Labels

When someone calls you handsome or gorgeous, your reaction is based on the labels you have for those words. In addition, the meaning you place on the words will be subject to other factors, like who said it, your relationship to that person, how they said it, and who else heard it. If it was someone you just started working for and in front of your new colleagues, would you find it offensive and patronizing? Would it cause you discomfort and dramatically reduce your ability to perform? On the other hand, if it was your spouse shortly after passionate sex, how would you respond? Would you see it as a turn-on or turn-off?

These are trivial examples and easily understood. However, what if the context wasn't as clear? What if the word handsome or gorgeous came from someone you work with in a private setting and you were massively attracted to that person? It gets murky. Equally, what if the word handsome or gorgeous came from someone you had only recently met socially? It gets equally murky. Consider if you had been conditioned to believe the word handsome or gorgeous has patronizing connotations, no matter what the context or tone. And consider if the other person believed something completely different. Perhaps they believed it was more of a general greeting and didn't hide any underlying intentions. Would things get harder for you if you get upset with a new boss and in a culture that uses the terms openly without any real associated meaning? And what of the person you had just met socially? How would you choose to respond? What if you responded negatively and defensively? Would you reduce your chances of a meaningful encounter and perhaps miss the opportunity to create a wonderful friendship or finally find love?

These many questions highlight the risks of being too black and white when it comes to perceptions.

Tribes

The idea that you would do anything for your tribe is noble in some ways and idiotic in others.

While being part of a tribe, or its darker relative, a cult, has its advantages, living in a bubble is very dangerous.

Tribes, or even cults, can be found in your family unit, your friend groups, your local communities, churches, political associations, or even subgroups within these. As time goes by, the needs, desires and aims of the tribe may get misaligned with what is important to you. The tribe's aims may no longer be fully aligned to what you might want. If you continue to blindly follow the instructions of the tribe, you might be taken in a direction which is not in your best interest.

Konstantin Kisin, author of *An Immigrant's Love Letter to the West*, *published in 2022*, sums up this concept beautifully in this posting on X:

'If you are on the left and think only the left has
good ideas and only the right has bad ideas,
you're dumb.

If you are on the right and think only the right has
good ideas and only the left has bad ideas, you're
also dumb.'

https://x.com/KonstantinKisin/status/1835025090372677650

Absolutes ('always' or 'never')

Not all labels hold you back, but you can achieve more engagement and richer experiences if you identify those that do. It is not easy to understand fully which labels are working for or against you.

COACHING CORNER: Identifying limiting labels

One method for identifying limiting labels is to observe how and when you use absolutes like 'always' or 'never'.

As an example, ask yourself, if any of these phrases feature in your conversations:

> 'I always think BLANK.'
> 'I always feel BLANK.'
> 'I always say BLANK.'
> 'I always do BLANK.'
> 'I always have BLANK.'
> 'I always buy BLANK.'
> 'I always wear BLANK.'

> Or you use 'never' with any of the examples above.

For each of these BLANKs, ask 'Why?' (i.e., 'Why do I always do BLANK?').

When you get the answer, reflect on the origins. See if you still feel the same now. If the answer includes an 'always' or 'never', think harder (i.e., 'I always wear blue, because I always have', isn't a reasonable answer). And look out for using someone or something else as the justification, (i.e., 'I always do it that way, because my father did it that way.'). This is a borrowed belief, which we will explore in chapter six.

It is likely that, if you can't provide your own answer to the why question, you are using a label for reasons that aren't your own. Finding the 'why' will help surface if the label is one that you might want to peel off, or the sign is one you want to take down.

Chapter 5: You don't have to

Agency is subtle.

Planes, trains, and buses

Have you ever found yourself feeling uncomfortable with the idea of engaging with the person next to you on public transport? Was there stress about starting a conversation? If you said nothing, did you ponder on your inaction for hours after? Perhaps you feared what would happen if you engaged. Perhaps you feared the person would be rude or boring. Were you relieved when the seat next to you was empty? Consider this: how often have others started conversations with you in similar situations?

The power of silence

They say, 'silence is golden'. Have you ever wondered why?

Silence is a tool that creates space for you and those around you. It creates the space to process what has been said and understand the meaning. Silence creates space to find new ideas and be creative. While powerful, using silence effectively isn't straightforward.

Perhaps you, like most, have been conditioned to think there is something wrong if you have nothing intelligent to say. Perhaps you believe that it is rude not to respond when spoken to. Perhaps you believe not responding suggests that you are not listening. The problem here is that everything that hits your ears causes thought, even if you are unaware of it. That thought could be related to formulating a response and understanding meaning. The words heard can even be a trigger of memories, good and bad, which in turn create thought and reflection. Unfortunately, making productive use of silence is not trivial.

It is all there between the words

There are three aspects that should be appreciated with respect to silence. The first is the importance of silence, even in well-established relationships. Secondly, silence isn't just about you—there is at least one other person to consider. And, finally, engagement is still a choice.

Using silence productively in relationships, is not 'the silent treatment'. Premeditated disengagement, when not being bullied or abused, is also a form of abuse. Purposefully refusing to acknowledge an approach or intentionally holding back, is not healthy for anyone involved. Holding things back and ignoring others, chews us up inside. It hurts the other parties, and it is a potentially damaging behaviour for our loved ones to have to witness.

For silence to work within relationships, of any kind, there needs to be a similar understanding of 'the gap'. The gap is the amount of time you leave between sentences. When you share something or tell a story, you do so with multiple sentences. You use small gaps to break the sentences and a long gap when you are finished. Those short gaps between sentences create both opportunities and discomfort. If the person listening typically talks faster and uses a smaller gap, they can frustrate the person talking because they 'butt in' before the line of thought is finished. Equally, when the person with the smaller gap is talking, they can get frustrated with what they perceive as lack of engagement. This is because they finish their story and expect a response but don't get one, so they feel they need to add more. This may not be the case, as the other person might be simply pausing between sentences.

Healthy engagement, therefore, involves being clear when your gap is being used inappropriately. Equally, you might need to shorten or lengthen your gap to accommodate people who don't appreciate this idea. Either way, you need to know your own gap, so you have a better chance of communicating effectively.

A sign of a healthy relationship is when all parties understand the needs relating to silence. When there is a good understanding of what is normal, communication thrives, even when nothing is being said. Those with a strong bond can sit for long periods of time in complete silence and feel totally at ease, even when facing each other.

Being clear about what you want helps when sitting next to someone you don't know. There are times when you want to enjoy your own thoughts. Then there are times when you would love to engage and learn something. However, it isn't clear from the offset which is the case and that can cause stress with those that feel it's rude not to speak. Something worth trying is to just smile and let the rest unfold. Do it immediately after you sit down or just as the other person does. The smile reduces your anxiety and theirs.

The smile is an invitation, but it doesn't provide a commitment. If you get a response that suggests an interest in conversation but not the confidence to start (i.e., you get a smile back), you simply add 'Hello' or 'Hi'. The conversation may or may not start. At least you tried. Trying helps relieve any guilt you may have carried in the past.

Smiling may not be enough. The key to starting confidently, is to have a method to get out. This is needed if you find yourself in a place where you don't really want to engage or find that you are not interested in what they want to share. The first method is simply to use silence. Saying nothing for a time often works. If that fails, start by acknowledging them, with something like 'That was really interesting, thank you for sharing.'. Make sure that you use past tense. Then, before they can respond, you add something like, 'Do you mind if I do some reading?' or 'Do you mind if I catch up on some sleep?'. It doesn't always work, but it's better than feeling guilty for hours, or days later.

Feeling worthy

The real lessons in your journey are not always obvious. Uncovering something is only the starting place. It often takes other interrelated events for the real meaning to be clear. Choosing not to speak to the person next to you, is about appreciating how to use silence, but it is also about something deeper. The fact is that you don't need to be friends with everyone. You can interact with most, to an acceptable degree, even if they don't like you. How you feel about yourself is far more important. Liking yourself is a bigger priority. You don't have to speak to the person next to you, however you can choose to.

Chapter 6: Return the borrowed beliefs

Agency doesn't just show up and can be given away, unknowingly.

Without question

You have probably been there, in a new place and being asked 'What do you do?'. It's a strange sort of a question really. While we know it means 'What kind of work do you do?', it can be an indicator of how authentic our behaviour is. For example, if you answered 'nurse' or 'engineer' or 'work for ABC technology company', you are not really answering the question of what you do. A better response might be 'I nurse people back to full health', or 'I build bridges', or 'help make smart phones.' These responses do help communicate something more about what you do, but it's still not fully realizing the potential of the question. You can get more from your relationships by being more open and more specific. For example, you could have said, 'I use my knowledge and empathetic nature to assist people in recovery so that they move back quickly to having rich and productive lives'. Or 'I bring creativity and ingenuity to building bridges for roadways so that people and goods can move across our country more efficiently.', or 'I use my attention to detail and dependability to help build devices which make the world a smaller place.' It is unlikely that anyone would use these latter responses in a first meeting with a stranger, but it begs the question as to why we filter and simplify how we communicate details about ourselves.

Picture a young man in the kitchen. He is cooking up a storm preparing the family dinner. He has the leg of lamb there in front of him.

His father peers over his shoulder and says, "Make sure you chop off the end of the leg before you stick it into the oven."

He turns to his dad and says, "What would I do that for?"

Dad replies, "Because that is how you cook a leg of lamb."

The young man isn't satisfied and questions him saying, "But why? How do you know?"

Dad is getting annoyed now and responds with, "Well, because my mum told me that was the way to do it."

The young man turns around and calls out, "Hey Gran, what's the story with cooking a leg of lamb?"

Gran comes over and says, "Well Ben, what I do is I chop off the end of the leg before I put it in the oven."

Ben replies, "But how do you know that is how to cook a leg of lamb?"

Gran responds with, "Because that is how my mother always did it."

So, Ben heads into the lounge and sits down on the sofa.

"Nanna?" he says.

Nanna replies, "What's up dear?"

Ben asks, "Dad and your daughter tell me that to cook a leg of lamb I need to cut off the end of the leg first."

Nanna grins, leans in and shares, "Well, dear, when I was your age, we lived in a small house and had a small oven. So, to fit the leg into the oven, I'd have to cut off the end."

Borrowed beliefs are beliefs that we adopt without question. We adopt them without understanding the assumptions and context on which they were formed. They obscure our options and therefore limit our choices. They can also become the basis on which we hide from our responsibilities.

Beliefs

Beliefs drive our behaviours, consciously, and unconsciously. We use beliefs to evaluate our experiences. Also, in a sense, beliefs encompass our goals in that, goals represent the desired future state of something that we value.

Beliefs address everything we do and experience. We have beliefs about what we eat, how we dress, and who we socialize with. Beliefs address the simplest of notions, like that of wearing matching socks. They also address more complex ideas of what we believe about how we greet people we have just met (i.e., should you shake hands firmly, go for one peck on the cheek or is it two, or even three, or what about a bear hug?)

COACHING CORNER: Understanding beliefs

Our beliefs drive how we work and play. For example, consider these questions:

1. What beliefs do you have relating to working away on your laptop, while in a meeting, or on a conference call?
2. What beliefs do you have about what are appropriate topics for conversations in the office, the home, or in the pub?
3. What beliefs do you have with respect to using phones while having dinner, minding the kids, or catching up with friends?

Beliefs also govern how we evaluate our experiences (i.e., we use them when we judge others on how they behave in a meeting or at the dinner table, or in passing in the hall, or not saying this or that).

The most interesting thing about beliefs, is that beliefs can be changed. In fact, they can be changed in an instant. All you need to do is revisit the assumptions or context from which the belief was formed.

For example, who thought football boots should be the same colour? Or on a more serious note, what beliefs were shattered the day the Twin Towers tumbled to the ground?

Beliefs can be changed, sometimes for the better, or sometimes not so much. At some stage you will have learned that trying to catch a ball was important because if you didn't, when the ball hit your chest, or head, it would have hurt. That belief may have served you for a period, perhaps until your fingers get hit trying to catch a hard ball. You may have then formed a new belief that you should not try to catch the ball, and you should get out of its way instead. That belief may not have served you any better if catching balls was important to being picked for the team.

License to compromise your potential

Learning about the 'borrowed' nature of some beliefs takes time and can come at great cost.

For example, being busy and making money, or just doing things for others, does not give you a license to compromise who you are and what you could be. Being busy is not a license to neglect your physical health (i.e., not exercise as much as you should, overeat, eat poorly, drink too much, and get insufficient sleep). Equally, it is not a licence to neglect your mental health (i.e., procrastinate about what you are going to do, binge scroll video reels, read little, and give in to material rewards). It is not a license to compromise on what you do as a son/daughter, brother/sister, girlfriend/boyfriend/spouse, parent, friend, or colleague (i.e., expect more of those around you than you should, expect to do less in other parts of your life, take more graces than you should, break promises, and let others down). Being busy does not give you the right to think, 'How dare you say I am cross, distracted, and never around! Everything that I am doing is being done for you!'. The only thing this attitude delivers is a life that falls short of your potential.

In his book *Talking to 'Crazy': How to Deal with the Irrational and Impossible People in your Life*, Mark Goulston explores the idea of being a martyr. This is the situation where people make a point of refusing to ask for help, even when they really need it. He explains that these people use guilt against others for not helping, even though they never give others enough opportunity to help. Mark explains that over time this behaviour makes others feel annoyed and exasperated. This helps explain why believing that 'busyness' is a license to compromise has the potential to really undo any good you might be trying to do. When making significant sacrifices for a good cause (i.e., your children, a charity, or even those you work for), you risk starting to feel you have a right to demand more than you should from those you are trying to help.

Over the last 100 or so years, the generations that shaped our world had it tough. Those that went through the World Wars and the Great Depression had a sort of desperation for any kind of work. With technological advancements and robotics that may become a reality for future generations too. Anyway, back then, there was likely a belief that any type of work, no matter what, was good, and a worthwhile pursuit. The kind of experiences at those times could also go part way to explaining the importance placed on paying the bills. Put in the context of people literally starving, together with the idea of any work is good work, could suggest that it is very important and worthwhile to be busy and paying the bills. One must wonder if the generations that shaped our world, compromised their wellbeing and who they were. It appears that they had balanced lives, even in the hardest of times. It appears that respect for themselves and others was still very much a part of how they lived.

To be clear, there is nothing wrong with being busy or making money. You must contribute and meet the needs of your commitments. The challenge comes when the 'being busy' part is not productive. The challenge comes when you focus on the busy part instead of the productive part. That gets in the way of you being the best person you can be. In theory, 'being busy' should equate to 'being productive'. In the past when most of us would have been growing, making, or moving things, being busy and being productive at the same time would be easily linked. Since we largely now work in the knowledge economy it has got a whole lot harder to equate busyness to productivity.

Peter Drucker wrote about the changing face of work in his 1967 book, *The Effective Executive*. He wrote that, 'the executive is ... expected to get the right things done.'. While he was writing about managers and leaders, his predictions can now be applied to most roles. We now have far greater choice of how we spend our time, and that choice directly affects our ability to be productive. When you choose the 'right things' (i.e., those aligned to who you want to be), you are productive. Unfortunately, you can be just as busy working away on the things that take you further away from who you want to be. If you are not consistently choosing the right ways to use your time and energy, you may still get there in the end, but it is unlikely that you will have travelled the easiest or shortest path.

The opposite of busyness is having a 'mind like water'. This is how David Allen describes it in his 2001 book, revised in 2015, titled *Getting Things Done. The Art of Stress-free Productivity*. Mind like water isn't about having an empty mind and doing nothing but staring blankly out of the window all day. Mind like water is about being in a perpetual flow state (i.e., the concept associated with Mihaly Csikszentmihalyi, which we explore in more detail in Chapter thirteen). This is where you are totally focused on what you are doing. You do that at the same time as being ready to effectively and efficiently handle any interruption or distraction. Eckhart Tolle says something similar in his 2001 book, *The Power of Now: A Guide to Spiritual Enlightenment*. Tolle suggests you should aim to be completely present in every moment, in everything you do, and in every interaction you have.

Limiting the choices

Beliefs are very important. To perform at your best, you need to accept that some beliefs will serve you, some will not, and some will be neutral. The key thing is that you just need to make sure that the beliefs you have are your own, are formed on your own values and traits, and not borrowed from someone or somewhere else.

A borrowed belief can obscure the options you allow yourself to see. It obscures options that may be aligned to your traits and your core values. This is because the borrowed belief is based on someone else's. By questioning the assumptions and context of a borrowed belief, you see other options which are more aligned to your values. You also see what will take better advantage of what you do well.

As well as obscuring options, borrowed beliefs have a certain comfort. This is dangerous. They have comfort because you can distance yourself from the responsibility of the outcomes of the behaviours and experiences resulting from the belief. You can numb yourself to the consequences of any associated actions. This has significant ramifications in all kinds of situations, from personal to professional.

Borrowed beliefs can be hard to find because their impact can be subtle. This is unlike the obvious beliefs that don't serve you (i.e., limiting beliefs). Limiting beliefs result in behaviours that don't help you feel good about yourself, don't build confidence, don't create enjoyment, don't create value, or don't have a positive impact on the world around you. The process of uncovering borrowed beliefs involves building a deeper awareness of your traits and values. You then use that awareness to question your behaviours and reactions. In doing so, you uncover beliefs that are obscuring options. You also see what is providing you with the excuse to hide from the consequences of your actions.

Handing over autonomy

COACHING CORNER: Lion in chains

Picture a room with a single door. The room represents a life experience. Picture yourself in that room ready to experience what the room has to offer.

Now what if a lion is dropped into the room. What would happen?

It is likely, all things being equal, that eventually the lion would get hungry and want to eat you. In that eventuality, what are your options? Most would choose to leave via the door, immediately. That would likely apply to every other time a lion is dropped into the room you are in.

What if there was a possibility that a lion might be dropped into every room, from that moment on. How would your experience of life pan out?

Dreadful and limited is the most likely answer. You wouldn't be able to stay or even enter any room. You'd miss every potential life experience.

Now, what if someone comes along and puts a chain on the lion and anchors it to the wall?

Well, you would be able to enter the room again. However, the lion would need to be chained down for every room you may enter.

This is not a good thing. It is a trojan horse.

If that other person is controlling the lion with chains, they are controlling you. They can choose to use chains or not. They can determine which room you can enter and which you cannot. Your potential for life experiences is controlled by them. You allow yourself to be the victim. Not a victim of the lion's hunger, but of the other person's will. You are allowing them to depower you. Your safety becomes dependent on somebody else putting chains on every lion.

You may counter that claim with the thought that you could learn to defend yourself against the lion. That might work but has risks. Another possibility might be that you learn to tame the lion. You could learn how to put chains on it yourself, so to speak. That way you could go into any room you like, regardless of whether there is a lion in there or not. You'd be safe without anyone else's intervention. You'd stay empowered. You would experience life to its fullest. You would have agency.

Changing beliefs

Often, when something is not the way you want it, you stick to what you know even though you know it causes you other problems. Changing is harder than it needs to be, when you let your beliefs get in the way of you seeing another, and perhaps better way, to do something.

The simple fact of the matter is that what makes us humans vastly different than all the other creatures we share this planet with, is that we change. We find better ways of doing things all the time.

Changing is simply the process of taking a new belief and using it instead of an old one.

COACHING CORNER: Changing a belief

The process of changing a belief is as follows:

1. When you find yourself disappointed with something you are doing or you perceive others are doing to you, you ask yourself, 'What do I believe to be important about this?'. Listen to the answers and then write these down.
2. Then for each thing you have written down, ask yourself these questions: 'What is important about this belief?', 'What does it give me?', 'Where does it put me?', 'Where is it used?' Write these answers down too.
3. For each of the subsequent answers, ask yourself 'What is important about this?', 'What is the context of this? What am I assuming?'.
4. Now, reflect on what occurs to you as you read what you have written.

If little comes of that reflection, check your memory for other times you have applied the same sort of logic and look for anything else related to assumptions and context. After this process, one of two things typically happens next. Either you find that you have borrowed this belief, or you no longer value the reasons on which the belief was based. In all cases you should either find a better way or find that you are now willing to search for one. Once you have clarified the reasons behind what you believe, it should be easier to move on.

Clarifying the context and assumptions on which your beliefs are based, or uncovering borrowed beliefs, does not solve all your problems. However, working from a set of beliefs which you understand and own, should make it that little bit easier to find the path that is truly of your own choosing, and that, enables agency.

Chapter 7: Show your cards

Agency involves risk.

Say or do it now

It is easier to clean up sooner than later, so say it or do it now. Small breaks are easier to repair than big ones. Admitting something after the fact takes a lot more effort than disclosure ahead of time. Holding onto concerns or suggestions drains your mental energy. The distraction caused in the short term by holding things inside, might be enough to take you off the rails and away from your true path. The longer you divert off course, the harder it will be to get back on track. That is not necessarily a bad thing. Often the shortest path is not the most scenic. However, you are shifting away from agency when you hold back on what is important to you in each moment.

The doorstep concept

The doorstep concept is the idea that you present a rosy picture of yourself from the doorstep outwards. The idea here is that the doorstep is as far as most people get (i.e., you stand at your doorstep talking to visitors and do not invite them in, or you interact with others outside the home but never invite them over). This behaviour is present in communities, churches, social circles, sports clubs, workplaces, and just about everywhere else. While this is a real physical behaviour in many cultures, it also applies to the filters people put up to protect themselves largely because of insecurities. The doorstep behaviour is evident when you hide your fears and real concerns, when you falsely portray yourself as being happy, and having a great relationship with your spouse and children. It is when you give the impression that you are part of a wonderful workplace or engaging social circle, when you are not. It is when you present a balanced and calm demeanour, when you are really burning inside. It is where you only show the rose-coloured view. It is where you project this image to everyone outside, yet when the doors are closed, things are different. You are withdrawn, angry, abrupt, unfocused, prone to shouting and yelling at loved ones, and susceptible to abusing yourself (i.e., with drugs, alcohol, and comfort foods).

The doorstep concept is also prevalent in those caught up in environments that focus on the material aspects and working every moment to have the nice clothes and big house with all the fine things.

When you allow the doorstep concept to rule your behaviours, you fail to appreciate the damage you are doing to yourself and those living around you.

Not starting from here

Where do you start from, when education systems, communities, and workplaces, only pretend to promote original and innovative thinking? Perhaps you have experienced push-back when sharing something that you felt was new and exciting. Maybe you have even been asked about the origin of a seemingly original idea. You might be asked who researched it, or who wrote about it. You might be asked about your credentials for having this thought. To have an original thought you are likely expected to have already written dozens of academic papers, toured fifty countries, spent ten years as a prisoner of war, or led an organization of fifty thousand employees.

These behaviours can have you thinking that because your life is 'normal', you couldn't possibly have anything original to add to the human experience.

It takes courage to share something new and exciting. Unfortunately, that courage gets whittled away if you get knocked back often enough. The courage gets replaced with a feeling of guilt that you haven't achieved enough to justify these crazy original thoughts you have.

So, where do you start?

A classic mistake in trying to fathom and overcome a challenge, is putting too much focus on where you wanted to be, not where you are. This humous little tale illustrates the point:

Imagine a city slicker, hopelessly lost in the countryside, who pulls over to ask a local farmer for directions to some distant town. The farmer, after a thoughtful pause, scratches his head and delivers the line: 'Well, if you want to get there, I wouldn't start from here.'.

The only place to start is right here—the very spot you find yourself in at any given moment. Adopting this approach doesn't suddenly move mountains. However, worrying about where to start, will certainly delay you from finding that clearer path.

Taking risks

With clarity on where to start, risks need to be taken. There is a philosophy that says hold your cards until you need to show them. It's based on the idea that if you have good cards, you should only show them at the right time to ensure you will win! That is good right? Not always.

When it comes to the cards that show what you are good at, you need to stop hiding them. There is little to lose in being yourself. You need to share what you do well. It is likely that you will find it hard to truly know what you are good at. It is, therefore, unrealistic to expect others to know.

A typical question in job interviews is, 'What are you good at?'. Struggling to answer that question in a concise manner could be due to conditioning. Perhaps you have been taught that you should not boast. This gets in the way of you looking at who you are and what you are good at. In answering the question, you might engage in a guessing game of what you think the other party wants to know. That may not serve you well. It will either annoy the interviewers or put you in a role that does not make optimal use of your strengths.

When you hide your true self, you must spend lots of energy managing the lie others adopt about you. That lie often results in letting others down. If you portray that you are fabulous, when you are not, others will expect that of you. It is inevitable then that you end up making apologies. Every time you use an apology, you erode the trust others have in you, and that you have in yourself.

What does the phrase 'I apologize' say about you when it's connected to lies and half-truths, like those resulting from the doorstep concept or holding your cards? What if someone was to turn it around and ask if you were remorseful or if forgiveness was being looked for? Perhaps you assume that you are letting someone down. Perhaps that isn't the case. Perhaps the other party already knows that you are not what you say you are, and therefore doesn't need an apology. Perhaps those words 'I apologize' are more about admitting to yourself that you are not who you portray. Perhaps apologizing just cements the damage you have done to the relationship. Clearly, there are techniques to avoid the apology (i.e., by saying 'I'm getting back to you now and here it is ... ' and not providing any excuses). A better approach might be to stop getting in a position where there is a need to apologize.

Showing your cards is not the same as publicising everything about yourself. Unfortunately, the world isn't a sugar-coated marshmallow land. You must put things in perspective and the right context. Stuff like date of birth, passwords, and bank account details aren't typically for sharing. There are plenty of opportunists who will take what you share publicly and use it for their own gain. No, you need to 'show' your cards to those that you trust, rather than 'publish' your cards to every man and his dog.

It does take effort to overcome the conditioning that tells us to project a false version of ourselves, not to share original crazy thoughts and to never take risks. However, the rewards are worth it. It is much easier to be open and honest when there are fewer secrets. Life gets easier when you stop living in a shadow of guilt about what you do well. Life gets easier when you have less to reconcile with. When the truth is out there, there is less to manage and control. There is more energy to focus on what you truly want.

PART 2:
BE A REALISTIC
OPTIMIST

Chapter 8: Take a spear!

Agency requires an optimistic but realistic approach.

Into the jungle

When you go into a jungle, take a spear! Hoping for the best but ignoring the dangers will only get you eaten. Equally, you must put yourself in the neighbourhood of danger on a regular basis, if you want to have a rich and engaging life. Never going into the jungle for fear of finding a sticky and uncomfortable end, holds you back. However, that doesn't mean you can avoid every danger or pitfall armed solely with a positive attitude. This idea is drawn from William Whitecloud's book, *The Last Shaman*, which is a wonderfully entertaining story of self-discovery.

Clearly, this isn't about going into a real jungle. No, this passage is about the jungle that is your daily life, working and playing. That jungle inevitably involves dealing with challenging situations, typically involving other people but also your own doubts and fears. For that, you need to equip yourself appropriately.

Lee Child's ex-military cop character Jack Reacher says, 'Hope for the best, plan for the worst.' Reacher faces all kinds of seemingly impossible situations. While his typical kit as he ventures around the US, involves no more than the clothes on his back, an expired passport, a bank card, and a toothbrush, he always pauses, assesses, and prepares for danger. At times that is simply a matter of sizing up his opponents and looking for their weaknesses. At other times, he enlists help from his network to gain access to the arsenal necessary to prevail.

When you simultaneously access and plan while looking positively at who you are and what you want, you are being a realistic optimist.

Getting through it

A great example that illustrates the benefits of being a realistic optimist is the story of United States military vice admiral, James B Stockdale. Also known as the Stockdale Paradox. Stockdale's story is told in the business leadership book by Jim Collins titled *Good to Great: Why Some Companies Make the Leap... And Others Don't*. Stockdale's story is striking because he spent eight years held captive during the Vietnam War. And not only did he survive when many others didn't, but he prevailed. He was not only an inspiration to his fellow prisoners, but he became an inspiration to many others when he got out of internment. He was tortured many times and really had no reason to believe he would survive the prison camp, to see his wife again. The key to his success was in how he pictured the outcome but balanced it with pragmatism. In his words:

'I never doubted not only that I would get out,

but also that I would prevail in the end and turn

the experience into the defining event of my life,

which, in retrospect, I would not trade.'

It was obvious that the pessimistic would flounder, however he also noted that the purely optimistic failed as well.

'They were the ones who said, "We're going to be out by Christmas." And Christmas would come, and Christmas would go. Then they'd say, "We're going to be out by Easter." And Easter would come, and Easter would go. And then Thanksgiving, and then it would be Christmas again. And they died of a broken heart.'

The pure optimists fail to appreciate the gravity of their situation and make allowances for it. To prevail, Stockdale had to simultaneously retain faith that he would prevail in the end, regardless of the difficulties, at the same time as confront the brutal truths of his reality.

Getting out of tight corners

To fully engage in the experiences, that you put yourself into, you need to pack the right stuff. This includes attitude and know how, in addition to material things. The right attitude, know how, tools and equipment give you options when you face a challenge. You can reach into your pack and get yourself out of a tight corner. If you don't carry what you need, you may have to turn back or take a less-than-ideal path. The potential for full engagement will be diminished. Arguably, the tools, equipment and know how are secondary to attitude, or mindset. In the absence of the right mindset, you risk misinterpreting the nature of the challenges.

Avoiding the bus

Another way to look at realistic optimism is that a pessimist won't cross the road, while an optimist will cross the road without awareness. The pessimist never gets anywhere, while the pure optimist is eventually going to end up under a bus. The realistic optimist crosses the road with awareness of the dangers and makes allowances for them (i.e., they look both ways before crossing the road).

Chapter 9: Choice without burden

It is a choice to have agency or not. The challenge is to know when you are leaning towards or away from it. That knowing is laden with burdens.

There is nothing wrong with me

The statement 'There is nothing wrong with me,' is both the truth and a naive misconception. Everyone has edges that could be a little smoother. Everyone has personality traits that need to be managed. Everyone has behaviours that don't serve them well. It's a fact of our human nature. However, the existence of flaws doesn't mean something is wrong. It is the opposite. To have flaws is normal. On the other hand, holding the belief that you are without flaws is naive. It is naive to think or say things like 'I don't have any problems to work on', or 'I don't need help with anything.' It is simply not true that you have no aspect to improve or learn about. There is always something you don't know or some experience you could learn from.

The belief that 'There is nothing wrong with me', implies that the problem lies with everyone else. It is a victim, closed or fixed mindset, and it is potentially very dangerous. When in safe circumstances, the attitude will just prevent you from learning new and wonderful things. It will simply hold you back from experiencing your full potential. However, if you get hold of some super-positive affirmations and buy into that way of thinking, the consequences can be fatal. Having the attitude that you are without fault and invincible at the same time is like walking into the mouth of a lion with your hands tied behind your back. You are totally exposed and unable to defend yourself.

Juggling complexity

Choice without burden is derived from the challenge of juggling complex layers of conflicting wants, needs, and commitments. That juggling involves trade-offs and the potential for conflict. The effort of that juggling could be thought of as a burden.

The burden is something like this. Firstly, you must carry the weight of where you find yourself right now. This relates to the impact of your past choices. Secondly, you must carry the weight of the future. This relates to the burden of the choices you have before you now.

Looking back

You will be often reminded of the burden of the choices you made in the past (i.e., the aspects in your world that you should continue to nurture or maintain). The obvious example being the emotional and financial support relating to children. Another example would be the bills that need to be paid to put food on the table and keep a roof over your head. Then of course, there are the commitments you have made to your family, friends, communities, colleagues, and customers, the job you took, the project you started, and the volunteering work you got involved in.

The burden from past decisions is optional. When you look negatively at these past choices, you feel like a victim of the situation; you try to find someone or something to blame. But when you look positively at the past choices, you see a different reality. You see the great things that you have done. You see what has taken place to bring you here. You see what has helped prepare the set of opportunities that lie before you. As an example, when you focus on the lack of personal time you get from the choice of having children or volunteering to fundraise for your community, you seek to blame. When you focus on the wonderful experiences, the friendship, the joy, and the learning opportunity you get from those same choices, you seek to embrace and engage.

Maintaining a positive attitude when looking into your past is not straightforward. When the challenges come hard and fast, it gets overwhelming. When you succumb to the overwhelm, you distance yourself from those choices and look for someone or something to blame.

The coping strategies are numerous. You can use friends and family, self-help books, motivational speakers, coaches and mentors, counsellors and psychotherapists. Each method has its place and each offer different benefits and drawbacks. Friends and family help look at things you are focused on in your immediate past. They provide a nice place to look for similar experiences and hopefully gain some insights. Self-help books and motivational speakers are a great way to see the types of experiences facing the wider community. They help you understand how others have managed those situations. Coaches and mentors help you take a different perspective on your experiences and bring you back to the present. They help you see how you will leverage past learning to move forward. Counsellors and psychotherapists help in explore conditioning and its impact on how you perceive the outcomes of your choices. Each method needs to bring you to a place where you own your past choices, and in doing so, release the burden.

Looking forward

In looking forward, the burden comes from the complexity and volume of the options before you. Making choices with a cluttered mind is like trying to prepare a big dinner for family and friends in a kitchen already jammed full of dirty dishes. There is a reduced sense of burden when you take control, get clear in your head about what you want and focus on one thing at a time. In the absence of burden, you get more done, and have more time to explore what it really means to choose your own path.

The white space

The sense of relief that comes when there is no burden, creates space. It gives you the opportunity to explore more about who you are and what it all means.

When you choose actions or put yourself in the way of experiences that are aligned with your true self, you are more inclined to feel enthusiastic and engaged, as well as have a better chance of being the person you want to be. A better understanding of who you are, helps you make better choices about where you put yourself and what you do when you are there. It helps you focus on how to best use your precious time and energy.

COACHING CORNER: *Assessing your focus*

The following model is helpful in assessing where your focus is as you look at the choices you have before you. The model has two questions. The first question is to ask yourself if you see meaning and purpose in every action you take and every experience you have. In other words, are your experiences free of doubt or burden? The second question is to ask yourself if you feel everything that you do and experience, is an optimal use of your time and energy. In other words, are you always in a calm state and getting what you want done in the time you want it to get done? Putting yes and no against these two questions gives you a place in the model.

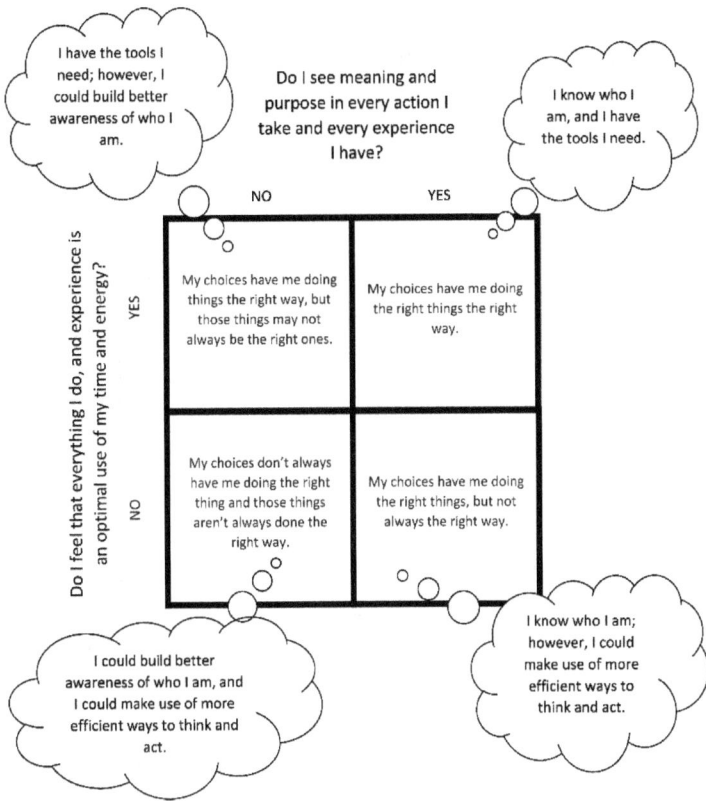

I have the tools I need; however, I could build better awareness of who I am.

Do I see meaning and purpose in every action I take and every experience I have?

I know who I am, and I have the tools I need.

NO   YES

Do I feel that everything I do, and experience is an optimal use of my time and energy?

YES

My choices have me doing things the right way, but those things may not always be the right ones.

My choices have me doing the right things the right way.

NO

My choices don't always have me doing the right thing and those things aren't always done the right way.

My choices have me doing the right things, but not always the right way.

I could build better awareness of who I am, and I could make use of more efficient ways to think and act.

I know who I am; however, I could make use of more efficient ways to think and act.

In the bottom-left corner, you are often finding yourself doing things that you don't feel serve you. You are likely finding that getting things done is hard and exhausting. In the bottom-right corner, you feel good about the things that you are doing, but you are still exhausted and continually playing catch-up. In the top-left corner you are doing things well and maintaining a good level of energy, but you don't feel you are doing enough to get ahead or serve others well. In the top-right corner, you are in flow, maintaining energy, and doing wonderful things for yourself and all those around you.

Where you are

Where you put yourself and what you do when you are there, is directly related to your ability to make good choices. Putting yourself in the right place has two extremes: the 'leave everything to chance' and the 'leave nothing to chance' approach.

When you take your chances, you don't get weighed down by what may or may not happen. You hope that you will be in the right place at the right time. You take the chance that you will be able to handle everything that comes at you. Using a game play analogy, you hope that you will be in the right place at the right time to catch the ball. You won't get bogged down by worrying what will happen when the ball comes in your direction. You won't spend time over thinking how you will catch it. You will congratulate yourself on being able to spontaneously react as needed to make that great catch. In taking this approach you are assuming that you will have enough warning to see the ball and adjust your position. Unfortunately, when things get complex, this approach has the risk of having you run all over the place trying to catch everything. This approach also runs the risk of completely missing the play altogether (i.e., not even being aware that a ball went past because of all the energy and attention being given to catching the others). On the other hand, this approach is a lot of fun and, owing to the pace, can give the impression of being very productive.

When you leave nothing to chance, you will spend lots of time and energy looking at everything that is going on and that is coming down the line. Using the game play analogy, you will systematically analyse every aspect of the field, the players and the stakes, to anticipate exactly where the balls will need catching. Then you will ensure that you, or someone else, is there to take the catch. Nothing gets through. In this approach, you are assuming that every ball must be caught. Unfortunately, as things get complex, this approach has the risk of you spending so much time in anticipating everything, that you never get onto the field of play. Furthermore, some plays will have a significant impact on the result and others won't. The difference between these minor and major plays is the level of importance. The analysis helps understand this, but it isn't the full solution. This is because the level of importance isn't always evident from the offset and only becomes clear once the play is underway. In other words, a lot of the time, you need to be on the field catching balls to really see what is happening in the game. That said, you do need to have a sense of the direction and intensity of the play in advance so you can put yourself in the general vicinity of where the balls will be landing.

Clearly, neither approach works in isolation. Both result in less than productive outcomes, wasted energy, and focus on too much of the wrong things. The balanced approach is simply about understanding the level of importance.

There is one final piece in this line of thought. There are times when you need to abandon the game altogether. If you are provided with an opportunity that gets in the way of your plans, you need to choose. Consider what you should do if you have made plans for an early start. Perhaps you have made a personal commitment to get some exercise first thing in the morning before starting work. However, the sun is shining and it's a perfect opportunity to meet friends, have a meal by the water and enjoy some beer or wine. That has the potential to get in the way of your plans for tomorrow. You need to assess what is important.

In work and play, the level of importance is down to one thing—core values. From the values come beliefs, and those beliefs drive behaviours and how you evaluate your experiences. So, whether you lean toward leave everything or nothing to chance, or face abandoning the play altogether, you still need to have a good understanding of what you see as important. We will explore core values further in chapter thirteen.

The pause

In facing down the choices that drive your journey, there is one other option you should consider. No matter how many choices are before you, there is always the choice to pause. Pausing isn't the same as avoiding agency. There is still engagement with choice in the pause. Continuing to process and consider the choices changes you and that changes your choices. Causality is in play (i.e., all that you think and do has an effect; things shift and change and so do your choices). Pausing simply implies you choose not to choose for a moment or two. Instead, you listen. As we will explore further in chapter eighteen, when you choose to pause and listen, you create the space for the answer to present itself to you.

Chapter 10: Perspective and absolutes

Ideally you would like to imagine that you are always doing your best at any given moment to be your best self. However, that isn't realistic because everything is relative, and nothing is absolute.

Troughs, peaks and hard places

To understand the impact of perspective, let's look at how you might climb a mountain. If you were asked to rate your chances in the valley at the start of the climb, you might look up, see the peak, and give yourself a goal. Perhaps you might say, 'My goal is to climb halfway.' Then as you progress, you might look up and see that you have climbed halfway to the peak you saw in the valley. At this point you might conclude 'I am done.' You might conclude that you can rest and take comfort in the knowledge that you have achieved your goal. You might boast and celebrate this success. From your starting perspective this is reasonable. Those who were with you in the valley will congratulate you and give you reason to feel successful. But what if the peak you saw was only a lower ridge on the slopes of the mountain? The true nature of the task would have been obscured by your perspective in the valley. If you share your delight with someone who knows the true scale of the mountain, you will look foolish. It is unlikely that you will get any recognition and that will be confusing for you.

Another way to look at perspective is to explore a rock. If you put yourself in the eyes of the rock, sitting on the ground observing yourself and your surrounds, you will see things moving past you, some fast, and some slow. You will observe yourself relative to these things.

You will see yourself as stable, unmoving, whole, complete, and wanting for nothing. You could say that you are at total ease with yourself and your place. What if you were now to step outside the eyes of the rock. What if you were to inspect the rock at an atomic level. What would you see? Well, you would see atoms, and particles moving rapidly. You would see a seemingly chaotic environment of many separate entities, all racing around the place, in constant movement. Now, what if you were to try to explain that to the rock. What would the rock think if you told it that it wasn't solid, whole, and static inside? The rock would struggle to conceive this as true, simply because its perspective doesn't allow it.

Embracing changes in perspective allows you to see progress and reassess your path. It also provides the opportunity to take another look at your priorities. When the mist clears and you see where you are, you can leverage it to build momentum. You can reset your milestones and drive on. Equally, when you look back down at the valley from the ridge, you see the valley in a new light. You can look at why you left the valley and consider the importance of what you are doing against that new perspective. Perhaps now that you are on the ridge, you realize it wasn't as exciting as you thought. You see what you valued about the valley. You can reframe that against why you are climbing the mountain.

Frame of reference

A further way to consider perspective is to experience the extreme or get sufficiently near it to reset your frame of reference. Many who sail will speak of 'getting their sea legs.' If you have ever got mildly seasick on a small boat, or ferry, you may form a fear of being at sea based on that experience. Perhaps during your initial experience, the imbalance across your senses was foreign and therefore unsettling. Perhaps your stomach turned, and you felt physically weak. In this state, if asked how bad this feeling is, you may answer that it is the worst feeling you've ever imagined.

The next time you are on a boat, perhaps your initial experience and fear of what could happen, causes you to immediately feel ill with even the slightest movement of the boat. Venture out on a boat, a few more times with this happening and you would be well on your way to cementing the belief that you get seasick, no matter the sea state.

Now, what would happen if you unwittingly found yourself at sea on a boat during a major storm? Perhaps the kind of storm that causes even the most sea hardened to struggle. If you'd built a belief around seasickness, in a major storm, the stress of what is coming would put your mind into chaos. The panic and over catastrophizing would cause your physical system to react. From there you'd get sick. And repeatedly, until even a sip of water would cause your system to revolt. While the body can go without water for three to four days, expelling fluids reduces your chances of survival. But here is the thing, even with the boat rocking and rolling, and you cuddling the toilet bowl, eventually the heaving will stop. When that happens, you can observe that you are still alive. When you acknowledge that fact, your mind creates a new reference point. Then as the seas calm and you get back to your feet, you take that new reference point with you. Fast forward to the next time that you are on a boat and things rock around a little, your mind will rationalise things differently. You will see that things could be a whole lot worse. The calmer mind and reduction in associated stress enables you to be more rational about the imbalance across your senses. You don't panic or over catastrophize. You breathe and hold things together.

While you have no choice in that you can't know what you don't know, you still need to be cautious not to frame every future moment and decision based on past perspectives or only what you see. You must be ready to reassess and rewrite your goals based on new perspectives as you move forward.

Grounding

Spending time with family and old friends provides the opportunity to remind yourself of who you are and where you came from. Reuniting with family or friends that you don't see regularly enables you to experience your previous self. This is useful but dangerous. The beliefs and behaviours that served you in the past, may not serve you now. Equally, you can benefit from being reminded of some aspects that might be better than what you now believe and how you currently behave. Those that you don't see very often will still hold the old version of you, as you of them. You fall back into language and manners that you used in their company, which is largely a good thing. It's comforting and enriching. It's the reason so many of us gather for yearly holiday celebrations. However, being drawn back into old limiting behaviours undoes any of the hard work you have done to change.

In dropping back into family or old friend comfort zones, not only do you risk behaving in your old limiting manner, but those around you may also treat you as they have always known you. This has two problems. Firstly, any changes you have made to better yourself might get suddenly undone, like giving up smoking, or cutting back on drinking, or taking up exercise. And secondly, anything new or different may not be tolerated or accepted. Like contrary belief systems or different approaches to managing complexity. Appreciating this is key to experiencing the good aspects of time with loved ones.

Furthermore, during these grounding gatherings we are reminded of two hard facts of life: children will eventually grow up and leave; and you will grow old. It is important, therefore, that you maintain personal space, friendships, and your intimate relationship. Putting everything into children isn't the best for them. They become too dependent, will struggle in life and will still leave, eventually (unless of course they stay, which might be even worse), In relation to getting old, some of those you care about may die before you. Family and friends may relocate and lose touch. You may change jobs and lose contact with colleagues. You will change over time and may no longer relate to those people already in your life. Some of those you hold dear will change over time and no longer want to be around you. And, most importantly, if you break off a long-term relationship, some of your mutual friends may take sides.

The learning, then, is to make friends where you can and don't get over reliant on any one circle (i.e., losing touch with your own friends and socializing only with your spouses' friends is a disaster waiting to happen). It puts you at risk of being alone at some point, and it is an awful burden to put on your spouse. Spreading the risk is a topic that we will explore further in chapter fifteen.

Absolutely not, but sometimes

Perspective both enables and inhibits your progress. The world and your place in it depend on several factors, not just what you see for yourself. You also must consider what others see. You take viewpoints from all those around you and from what you experience. Some of what you experience is designed to manipulate you, like advertising.

Another way to consider perspective is that it is a set of measures you create to assess your place and progress. The key is to create the best measures for you, not others. When the measures are derived from someone else's perspective you run the risk of derailing. You run the risk of progressing toward someone else's version of what is good for you, not your own. The tell-tale signs, as explored in chapter four and chapter six, involve the use of absolutes. Using terms like 'only', 'never' or 'always' indicate a belief that may not be derived from your own perspective. Some examples include: 'I always go to the gym on Mondays and Wednesdays', 'I only eat cake on special occasions', 'I never drink mid- week', 'I always call my parents on Sundays', 'I never think bad of anyone', and 'I only binge watch videos for an hour a day'. Views expressed as an absolute are rarely true. There is only one absolute fact and that is that there are no absolutes in truth, only varying degrees of perspective.

By removing the absolute, you reduce the guilt that might surface. This also applies to other vices, like drinking alcohol, or smoking or playing computer games. It becomes a better way of seeing what works. Some examples include, 'sometimes I exercise and sometimes I do not', 'sometimes I eat well and sometimes I do not', and 'sometimes I go to the gym, sometimes I do not'. Another subtle variation of this theme is the contradiction. For example, you could also use 'I never eat fried chicken, apart from when I do', or 'I always go to the gym daily, apart from when I do not', It still works.

Living with absolutes increases the potential for over-confidence as well as hiding in the comforts. You orientate yourself toward fear and bring on unnecessary stress. All that holds you back. It assumes you are already at the end of the line. It assumes you have already reached the top of the mountain. It assumes you have already reached your potential.

Avoiding absolutes opens you up to the potential for learning. When you leave a space for being wrong, you have a better chance of seeing the new perspective. When you remove the need to always or never do something or not do something, you appreciate the sunshine, and brightness as well as the mist, the clouds, and the gloom. You see it all as potential for a new perspective.

There is no witch

The story of Hansel and Gretel, popularized by the Brothers Grimm, offers deeper insights into perspective, when viewed through the lens of symbolism.

In the tale, a poor couple, representing the masculine (order) and feminine (chaos) principles, fearing starvation, leave their children, Hansel and Gretel, in the woods to die. Hansel and Gretel, symbolizing younger, less corrupted versions of these principles, overhear this plan and attempt to return home but end up lost. They stumble upon a candy house, which belongs to a witch — an embodiment of corruption and our darker selves.

The narrative begins with scarcity, symbolizing not just physical need but also a lack of purpose, leading to corruption. This corruption blocks curiosity, growth, and compassion, causing society to cling to outdated structures, represented by the parents' decision to abandon the children.

The children's first attempt to return home illustrates both their innocence and society's deep corruption. The second attempt shows youthful overconfidence, suggesting they must learn and grow before returning to safety.

Discovering the witch's house represents the naive search for utopia, where all needs are met effortlessly. However, this leads them into danger, as the candy house signifies entitlement and false ideals detached from the reality of hard work.

Gretel, consumed by order, and Hansel, by chaos, the opposites of their innate tendencies, both fall into traps of their own making. Gretel, always working, represents an imbalance towards order, while Hansel, neglecting himself, symbolizes a life wasted in chaos.

The witch's defeat by Gretel signifies self-awareness and overcoming one's lesser self. Gretel's actions help Hansel recognize his own entrapment, leading to their liberation from these personal cages.

Upon returning home, they find the woman dead and the man heartbroken, symbolizing the end of an old, corrupt society. The pearls and stones they bring back from the witch's house represent the wisdom gained from their ordeal, essential for rebuilding society with balance.

The journey back, including crossing a river with a swan's help, signifies the individual path of wisdom each must tread before achieving harmony. With the old chaos gone and only remnants of order left, Hansel and Gretel, as youthful embodiments of order and chaos, can now work towards restoring balance using the wisdom they've acquired.

This story begs the question, are you living in balance, or are you trapped in your own candy house of order or chaos?

Perspective risk

While flawed, your perspective is still fundamental to making decisions. To choose your own path, you need to make decisions and those must be made with some level of certainty. Even when you accepted that an obsession with certainty holds you back, you still must make decisions. Decisions are impossible if everything is an unknown. The trick is to test your perspective so that the level of trust is enough. That process is straightforward. you simply need to test your assumptions and look for gaps.

COACHING CORNER: Testing your perspective.

The process to test your perspective is as follows: First, write down everything you know about where you are, how you feel, what you see, and whatever else you think will be true when you reach your goal. The list from our earlier mountain climbing story might look something like this:

- I am here, with my two feet planted in the valley.
- There are trees and rivers here.
- There will be a wonderful view from the top of the mountain.
- I can see only one way out of this valley.
- I can see the top of the mountain, up there beyond the tree line.
- I will feel brilliant at the top of the mountain.
- I will see the whole valley from up there.
- I have all that I need to get started.
- I will have more options (i.e., paths to take), from the top of the mountain.
- I can see the path I must take, from here to there.

The next step is to get help or use a very critical eye and review the list. Look for things you don't really know for certain. There are lots of examples in this list (i.e., 'only one way out of this valley', 'I can see the top of the mountain' and 'I will have more options'). At this point you might find some other things to add to the list, like 'I don't know what it is like being on top of the mountain I see before me' and 'I don't know if the paths I see from the top of the mountain will be for me'. From there, if anything is obviously wrong, you might rethink the plan. Otherwise, you will set forth, bringing the list with you. Along the way, you might take moments to reflect on this list again. You might check for things that are new, things that were wrong, and things that are still true.

When you manage it, instead of your perspective being a crutch or something to blame, it becomes a platform to learn and grow from.

Chapter 11: Fail well

Agency is a process of self-correction.

Success driven

Childhood conditioning, education, and workplaces rarely include preparation for failure. We are taught to aim for the good grades, to win the competition, and to get that top job. The focus is on how you achieve success.

While there is not anything wrong with reaching the top, it is lifting yourself up when you hit the bottom that causes difficulty. We are rarely taught how to use failure properly, to learn from it, to grow stronger from it, to become more resilient. This lacking in the skills needed to cope with life's challenges, runs the risk of driving our existence to a dark place. Things are far too complex to suggest this failing rests in any single place. As educators, as parents, as colleagues and friends, everyone shoulders that responsibility. They all have a role to play in helping each other understand failure. In doing so they can extract the learning and become stronger.

Imagine a world where people did what they say by when they said they'd do it, without needing to be reminded. Imagine a world where people actively renegotiated their commitments sufficiently ahead of time rather than being reminded of them when they'd already failed to deliver on them. Imagine a world where there was not a need to make allowances for those that rarely deliver on what they promise. What would that world be like? How much less mental energy would that world need? What other things could be accomplished in that world?

Would that world be too perfect, too contrived, and too easy? Would you want that world? After all, is it not the bumps and wobbles in your journey that create the best opportunities for learning and growth?

Embracing the wobble

You may feel aligned. You may feel you have clarity. You may have confidence in the effectiveness and efficiency of your systems and ways of getting things done. You may feel on top of your exercise, eating, sleeping, relationships, and career. No matter how good things are going, you always experience wobbles.

Watch a professional sports person performing and you may notice they are constantly correcting. Watch someone that is good with a skateboard and the same things happen. You may even know the feeling. At one moment you are cruising: the wind is in your hair, you are looking and feeling good. Life is perfect. However, you are moving and by moving you are subject to constantly changing conditions: a stone, a break in the pavement, a gust of wind, something catching your eye, a distracting thought. Whatever it is, it will cause a wobble. What happens next is all too common. You don't become aware of the change in the conditions until it's too late. You over correct and end up on your arse. What is worse is that the faster you go, the harder it is to correct the wobble and the harder the fall. Life is just like that.

The trick is to get familiar with the wobble. Get used to sensing it coming on. Get practiced at correcting and adjusting. Get to know how to change direction, balance, and even speed. And most importantly, get used to taking falls. You can't always catch the wobble. Sometimes, you are going to take a fall. However, a fall is a good thing. It helps you see where your boundaries are at now. Over time, you may find you can pick up more speed, take more risks. The wobbles become less frequent, and you get better at handling them when they do occur, even at speed.

Agency by its nature includes the noticing and the correcting. Agency is learning to learn from the wobbles.

Built in know-how

Relationships that last do so because the know-how to get out of trouble has been built in. The skills to navigate through and out of stormy waters is part and parcel of the deal. As explored in chapter three, things don't go so well when there is insufficient investment in preparation and maintenance in the foundations of a relationship. Things fail when we lack the knowledge of how to leverage the downturns to create upward momentum.

Failed marriages turn ugly when the know-how to sail through troubled waters is lacking. While it can be, most breakups never suddenly end, they crumbled to pieces over time. While plenty of effort might be made to keep things together, the relationship turns into a battle zone when the preparation and investment isn't there.

Often breakups are justified on the basis of 'incompatibility'. This is rarely the full truth, especially when the relationship fails after a prolonged period. The truth is typically more complex. A demise after such a long period can't be simply explained through incompatibility. That reasoning doesn't account for all the wonderful times.

You might start out in an optimistic place. You might be highly motivated. Perhaps you feel you could achieve anything just with a positive attitude and affirmations. Perhaps that state of mind is intoxicating to those you meet. You both then get caught up in the myth that you had romanticized. This is not ideal. It might produce some great times and interesting experiences, and it might be very productive in terms of creating a family, but if it is not based on truth, it may all unravel, perhaps spectacularly. Over time, things get realigned with your truer self. When that happens, there is not much left to be the basis of a relationship. Unfortunately, this realisation can come too late.

Perhaps there are other factors working against you. Trying to parent at the best of times is challenging, but with a flawed foundation in the relationship it is nearly impossible. Being a parent on top of all the other financial and non-financial commitments puts serious demands on your focus and energy. With what precious time is left, surrendering becomes a far more attractive proposition than sharing a meal, a glass of wine, some banter, or anything close to intimacy. There is absolutely no time left for repair. Without the preparation and ongoing investment, a marriage becomes a largely repetitive and uninspiring existence. Furthermore, the growing process can bring about more truth, which in turn can cause further conflict. If there is lacking in the foundations in the relationship, to turn mistakes and challenges into lessons, things will eventually unravel.

The right mindset

> 'Success is stumbling from failure to failure with no loss of enthusiasm.' – Winston Churchill

> 'Only those who dare to fail greatly can ever achieve greatly.' – Robert F. Kennedy

> 'If you're not prepared to be wrong, you'll never come up with anything original.' – Ken Robinson

Failing well is the idea that you learn something from your mistakes. The potential for learning exists all the time, in every minute, hour, day, or week. It doesn't need to be major life events.

Failing well isn't a new thing. Eastern teaching points to the beginner's mindset. We have access to mountains of material on the growth and learner's mindset. It all points to the same path. Failing without learning reduces our ability to build resilience. The wrong mindset holds us back and can put us in harm's way. The opposite is the belief that there is always more to uncover about ourselves and our context.

The most wonderful thing about the learner's mindset is that it is built in already. You just need to use it. A baby doesn't give up when failing to stand on two feet causes a sharp pain in the behind. The toddler doesn't stop trying to run when the sofa corner brings the show to a halt. Without focus, over time you risk losing interest in learning. They say you can't teach an old dog new tricks. You will likely see examples around you, where excessive pride or over-confidence blinds people from the facts of their situation, often leading to less-than-ideal experiences or even tragic consequences. You will have experienced or know of those who have fallen out of employment because their skills become redundant as the world changes. You will see complacency in day-to-day existence where the room for learning is eliminated as entertainment takes over discretionary time. The truth is that you can learn, once you remember where you started.

Failing well is a gradual process. The time to learn that fire burns is not as you step into the path of a lava flow. Feeling the heat from a birthday candle is a better place to start. Building knowledge of what is good and not so good for you in a physical sense applies equally to your internal world. Just like strengthening your arm, leg, and core muscles through exercise and workouts, you need to learn gradually. You need to stretch but not tear the muscle for it to strengthen. The same goes with how you learn about math, science, writing, or any number of academic topics. Equally, you must learn gradually about yourself. You must slowly peel back the layers of your understanding of who you are and what you are capable of. Major emotional trauma is fertile ground for learning; however, you risk being completely broken by it. Experiencing disappointment and hurt is a better place to start. Learning gradually about managing emotions increases your ability to cope with and recover from life's challenges. If you can't properly rationalize things that aren't where you expect them, you run the risk of falling hard, which can result in tragedy.

Breaking free

Fred Kofman, in his book, *Conscious Business: How to Build Value Through Values*, provides wonderful insights for breaking free of limiting beliefs. His approach helps in moving away from the victim mentality, where one perceives themselves as a victim despite no real crime or harm. It applies equally to the closed or fixed mindset, where one is hellbent on staying with a particular direction.

COACHING CORNER: *Kofman's approach*:

Here is a summary of Kofman's approach:

Stage 1 - Recognize where you are trapped in a victim or fixed mindset. Pay attention to words that focus on elements that are out of your control (i.e., listen to when you refer to other parties as being the problem). Stay curious and consider the challenge you are facing and how you responded. Try avoiding dwelling in this exploration, just pay attention to when you blame others.

Stage 2 – Disarm the blame. Consider how would the other parties explain this situation. Consider to what extent you are responsible for the situation, even if just a fraction. Ask yourself, 'How is this working out for me?'. Try to stay focused on the story or the problem and not the relationship with the story. Avoid dwelling too deeply on what happened to you.

Stage 3 – Embrace agency: Consider what you could do differently, how you could be challenged, and what are you willing to try.

In general, avoid jumping to solutions before exploring what you can control.

The retrospective

COACHING CORNER: Retrospectives

Best practice in many modern work methodologies makes use of a straightforward review to learn and grow, at the completion of a piece of work. These reviews occur no matter the outcome (i.e., successful, or otherwise). These reviews typically involve the full team and take a brief period compared to the aspect under review. For example, in the Agile Scrum methodology for developing software, a typical cycle lasts 2–3 weeks. One aspect at the end of the cycle is the retrospective review. It usually takes no more than 30–40 minutes. The key with this, and all forms of retrospectives, is that the learning potential does not get in the way of the momentum. Therefore, the reviews are short, focused, and done in a specific manner. The questions asked at these reviews are positive and focused on learning.

Here are some examples:

1. What worked—what can we be proud of?
2. What did not work—what will we stop doing?
3. What could we try—what unexplored aspect might help?

The process intentionally avoids 'why' questions. These types of questions invoke the need to find causes only and defocus the attention on solutions. A well-formed 'what' question will inherently involve thinking about the cause but bring focus to the solution.

Before answering the 'What', our brains automatically join the dots on the causes to understand what did or did not happen. With the correct 'What' question, our minds do not dwell on the causes.

A variation of these questions works well for personal retrospectives. For example, after failing at something, or feeling disappointed or being let down, you might ask yourself:

1. 'What do I have—what can I be proud of or grateful for?'
2. 'What isn't working— what should I stop doing?'
3. 'What could I try—what steps could I take now or next time that might work better?'

Life is a wonderful experience when you venture into the jungle. To survive the jungle, you need to prepare yourself without over-cooking it. Half the fun is the frantic search for a tree to climb when the spear breaks.

PART 3:
PUT YOURSELF
FIRST

Chapter 12: Juggling life's priorities

Agency isn't about being a martyr.

Nurturing

Most of us find it hard to openly commit to putting ourselves first. This is especially true for parents, or carers. Observe the look of horror on people's faces if you suggest that you prioritize yourself over everything and everyone else.

At an early age you were likely taught that you should put others before yourself, especially those you love, care for, and the vulnerable. Unfortunately, if you don't look after yourself, you are limiting your ability to help others. When you nurture your own mental and physical wellbeing, you are better placed to nurture the wellbeing of those you care about. When you nurture and use your strengths well, you radiate your potential to all those around you. It is through that process that you help others with their own wellbeing. For most, that is a primary source of meaning. So, take note when the airline attendant tells you to put your own oxygen mask on first before helping others.

In this book, we are exploring how the choices you make create your experience and bring you closer to a truer existence. Through those choices and resulting experiences, there is one choice that needs more attention than others.

Your experience is greatly impacted by who you choose to have join you on the journey. However, there is one person who is coming along, whether you like it or not. There is one person you cannot choose to ignore, move away from, or sack. No matter what family, work, or social relationships you find yourself operating within, there is one person that will always be there in every one of those relationships. At four a.m. in the morning when all is quiet, there is only one person you can truly count on to answer the call. It is a true pickle because that person needs the support too. That person is YOU, so you had better get to like that person and take care of him/her, and you had better do an awesome job of it! The alternative is a sad and devastating eventuality to all those wonderful people that choose to be on your journey with you.

Most parents will easily find examples where their health and wellbeing has been sacrificed for the benefit of their children. Carers will have a similar story. Perhaps they do no exercise, have farcical engagement with their spouse, have no time with friends or extended family and make zero real downtime for themselves. Unfortunately, this strategy only works in the short term. Over time, the clothes get tighter, a good night's sleep seems like a distant memory, smiles are only seen in old photos, and good humour is non-existent. Over time it gets harder and harder to find the energy needed to give your all to those you love and care for. This level of sacrifice put you in the back seat of Thelma and Louise's convertible, roaring toward the cliff edge.

Juggling life

The concept of 'work-life balance' gets a lot of attention. The implication of the phrase is that 'work' and 'life' are somehow separate or opposing concepts. While you will likely appreciate that this concept is really about boundaries, trading one off against the other is not realistic as they are connected and overlap.

There are many aspects to life. Some require lots of attention and some cause discomfort, and then there are lots of aspects that cause joy and pleasure. Doing life well is not about balancing. That is because, life is a juggling act.

If you consider juggling balls, the key is to have strong arms and to master their movement, so that it becomes automatic, so they are in flow. Once you've mastered that, you no longer need to focus on where your arms are at. You simply focus on where the balls are, or bowling pins, or machetes. Mastering the juggling act of life is the same thing. You need to be strong mentally and physically and you need to automate as much as possible. With the mechanics in flow, your mind is free to focus on where you are.

Burnout

Burnout is a symptom not the cause. It is a symptom of the prolonged absence of flow. It is a situation, over a prolonged period, where our juggling is inefficient or simply not happening. As we will explore further below, flow is where there is the right balance between the skills we have for coping with the challenges at hand and the difficulty, complexity and volume of those challenges. If there is imbalance for too long, we suffer overwhelm, we get disillusioned and suffer in motivation. This is where burnout shows up.

Chronic stress

'It is not what happens to you, but how you react to it that matters' - Epictetus

Chronic stress, excessive worry, overthinking, preoccupation and other related derailing conditions aren't things to be taken lightly. Long term resolution will likely involve therapy/counselling. In the short-term, however, you face a choice. You can choose to allow these situations to distract and overwhelm you. Alternatively, you can choose to manage the moment and engage with what is in your immediate control. The foundations needed for this latter choice are part of what you will find within the next four chapters. You will find specific techniques for managing the distracting nature of negative thoughts in chapter twenty.

Bouncing forward

Juggling life is encapsulated in the concept of resilience.

You will likely be familiar with the notion of resilience as having the ability to 'bounce back' from a major setback or loss. While it is that, it is also the ability to thrive through those challenging times. It is having the skills to 'bounce forward'. Often, we think of resilience as something you either have or don't have. This is not the case. As presented by Shelley Crawford in her research, resilience is something you build, gradually over time, through failing well as explored in chapter eleven. While you will learn from major emotional trauma, it can also send you into crazy land. The best approach to building resilience is through learning from experiences which involve strong emotions, both positive and negative.

You have likely experienced others who seem calm and at ease in the face of major setbacks. They do have high levels of resilience, but whether through conditioning, or study, it was learnt. This is wonderful news. To master the movement that is necessary to juggle life well (i.e., build resilience), you need to tune how you think, how you feel, how you socialize, and the physical aspects of your personal experience. These four aspects are the focus of the four chapters that follow. There is a fifth dimension. That dimension relates to how you connect everything. This dimension is explored throughout this book and summarized in the final chapter.

Chapter 13: Thinking it through

Agency needs thought.

Self-talk

A wonderful representation of self-talk is done by Johnny Depp in character as Jack Sparrow in the *Pirates of the Caribbean* movies. It's when he talks to his good and bad side. Two miniature Jacks, in all their pirate glory, appear on either shoulder then whisper into his ear. One 'mini-Jack' is encouraging him to think of himself. The other is encouraging him to look at the wider consequences. It's a wonderful depiction of the constant conversation that goes on between the ears. However, there is a flaw in Jack Sparrow's council. The flaw is that it is too simplistic. It is black and white. As explored in chapter ten, there are no absolutes. We typically have many variations of our 'mini-me' floating around our heads, all talking, often at the same time.

Self-talk appraises everything you see, hear, smell, touch, and taste. It also appraises your feelings and memories. That appraisal process influences how you act or react to how you experience the world. Even when you are talking to someone else, getting their advice, you are still interpreting and reframing what they share into your own version of the truth. You form all number of associations with everything that comes to you.

Have you ever been asked 'what are you thinking?' What happened? Did you have an answer? Or did you reply with 'nothing' or something to that effect. Was that the truth? The fact is that we are always thinking, whether we are conscious of it or not. Even as you read this paragraph, you are processing and thinking, trying to understand it and relate it to your own experience. Interestingly, the 'what are you thinking' question is impossible to answer. This is because the question interrupts the thinking process. After the interruption, all we can generally think about is why have we been asked the question. For some, the internal defences go up and what happens next is of no value to you or the person asking. We will get to that further in this chapter. For now, let's accept that we are always thinking. The key to agency is to be in control of our thinking, when we need to.

Set the stage

While we are always thinking, our mind has a serious limitation that can severely hamper our ability to perform. The limitation is simply in the way we think. As with all limitations, understanding them allows us to manage or negate the impact on our ability to perform at our best.

David Rock's metaphor of the prefrontal cortex, helps explain this limitation. In his book *Your Brain at Work: Strategies for Overcoming Distraction, Regaining Focus, and Working Smarter All Day Long*, Rock presents the idea of a theatre. The stage of the theatre is the prefrontal cortex and our short-term memory. It is the part of the brain that we use for thought. To think we bring actors onto the stage and have them interact. The actors can come from outside the theatre (i.e., the outer world) or the audience (i.e., our inner world). The inner world is our memories.

To use our memories in our thinking we need to find them and bring them up onto the stage. The order of the seating of the audience represents how recently we have had that memory on the stage, i.e., in our conscious thoughts. Older memories will find themselves way up the back in the dark and may take some time to be found. This has two implications. Firstly, it can take time to get an answer to a question and secondly, answers and reminders can be landed on stage at any time and interrupt our thinking. This helps explain why that movie name, that escaped you during dinner over the weekend, suddenly pops into your mind during a meeting on Tuesday morning. It also explains how at seemingly random moments, we get reminded of things that need doing, and not always when we can do something about them. The mind will throw things on stage, independently of what we want to focus on, so that we don't forget. In a sense, the mind can interrupt itself.

To make sense of our thoughts we need the actors on the stage long enough for us to interact with them and make decisions. And here is the clincher—while the seated area of the theatre is infinitely large, the stage is not. In fact, the stage can only hold focus on one thing at a time. This fact doesn't sit well with those who think they are good at multi-tasking. Unfortunately, they are deceived. The truth is that we can only focus our conscious thought on one thing at any one time. There can be the appearance of multi-tasking, but that is simply the activity of swapping things on and off the stage. Someone who can quickly swap actors on and off the stage may be a good multi-tasker. However, not giving the actors enough time on stage also translates to poor decision making.

When you take an active role in how you use your 'stage' you have a better chance of ensuring it is used for the things that bring you closer to where you want to be, not further away.

Another way of thinking of this is a theatre production without a director. When there is no director, the production depends entirely on the quality of the script and the ability of the actors and support crew to 'play along nicely'. This idea also assumes a nice and controlled environment, where the audience behaves, and the stage doors are well managed. The doors are the million and one ways that you can receive new information. Even if you were to lock yourself away in a dark, sound-proofed, padded room with no devices, you simply can't escape your thoughts. The director then, in terms of your own mind, is the part of your conscious mind which is aware of your thoughts and where your attention is.

The hijack

Even if you aspire to hold yourself up to a high standard in how you present yourself and interact with the world, it doesn't always happen. There are times when you will feel out of control, or wish you did something different in certain moments. At these times it will feel like you are wrestling with your own mind. Using the theatre metaphor, it will feel like a guest director has stepped in with a completely new script and is reorganizing things to their liking, not yours. Thankfully, there is an explanation for why this happens.

Our brains can be thought of in terms of three main parts, the lower or reptilian part, the middle, or mammalian part and the upper or human part.

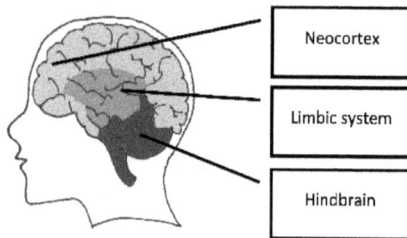

Neocortex

Limbic system

Hindbrain

Each is aptly named because of the characteristic of each that we share with said creatures.

The reptilian part, or as it's known more technically, the hindbrain, includes the brain stem, and our autonomic nervous system. This part of the brain is associated with 'freeze, fight or flight' responses. This lower part is concerned with survival. It is known as the reptilian part because its functions are shared with reptiles and all other creatures that have evolved along the same path.

The middle or mammalian part, also known as the limbic system, is our memory storage and the emotional centre. It is here within this middle part that we have emotions and feelings, an essential aspect to bonding with each other and, as it is with all mammals, bonding with our young. This is our theatre seating.

The upper part, the human part, also known as the neocortex, is the thinking, or rational part of our brain. It is within this part of the brain that we process and evaluate the inputs we receive and decide what to do about them. This is our theatre stage.

Connected to the three parts of the brain is the amygdala. While small, the amygdala plays a particularly important role. Its primary purpose is to help us survive. It is a kind of radar, which has the job of looking out for threats. How it works is that it takes the inputs generated from our senses and events around us and searches our memories for close matching patterns. Once it finds a close enough match it can take over the functions of the brain and force that memory onto our actions. The logic being that if we are still alive the response must have worked in the past.

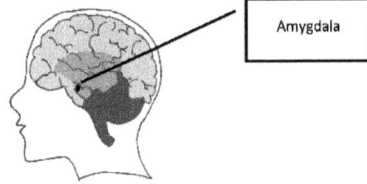

Amygdala

Having a fast and efficient way to react is good if our senses have picked up a fast-approaching ball on the pitch that needs to be caught or a dog dashing out in front of the car that needs to be avoided.

This capability is not so good if our sensors have picked up an action, comment, and tone that has caused us pain in the past. It is not so good because it is rare that past situations of this nature are the same as the present. And in most personal and professional situations, actions and comments from others require thought before a response is warranted. However, if the amygdala is permitted to do its job, it will block out the upper brain and take over. The response and action will be driven from things we have experienced in the past. The amygdala has no ability to reassess the present or adapt. It is purely a reactive function and executes what worked previously.

This is the Amygdala Hijack: a situation where we act based on what happened in the past and completely stop considering anything new or different and anything specific to the present moment. Amygdala Hijack is a term coined by Daniel Goleman in his 1996 book, *Emotional Intelligence: Why It Can Matter More Than IQ*.

Once in a hijack, we will be irrational. We will not be able to communicate effectively. We may withdraw, we may get aggressive and will do and say things that we wouldn't, if we had the opportunity to think about it.

Another worrying thing about the hijack is that it can last for prolonged periods. The hijack typically lasts for a few moments, but it also can last for hours, days, weeks. This happens when the emotion to memory association is so strong that we accept it as being normal. This blocks our rational thinking for extended periods of time. It is not that we are irrational from that moment on, it is just that we make a habit of applying the memory instantly. We get so familiar with the pattern and response, that it becomes our default behaviour. We can operate quite rationally for most of the time, but the instant the situation arises again we go straight into that irrational place.

We all have experienced an amygdala hijack. We have experienced them ourselves and we will be subject to others experiencing them. A child's tantrum, someone losing their temper, or someone going silent in a meeting are all examples. There are plenty more. It affects both personal and professional aspects of our lives. However, there is hope! The amygdala hijack can be prevented. We can learn to manage our thinking and avoid it entirely.

The upper, or thinking, part of our brain can shut down the amygdala before it can take over. Inputs from our senses and events around us are simultaneously provided to both the amygdala and the upper brain. In the upper brain we can then consider the situation and choose what to do about it. So, the key is to catch the associated emotion and start thinking consciously about it before the amygdala gets up to speed. This conscious thought will quieten the amygdala and leave our rational side in control. Quietening the amygdala is not hard, however there are two conditions that must be met. We will look at both, later in the chapter.

Flow

The concept of 'flow', or the 'flow state', is largely associated with the work of Mihaly Csikszentmihalyi, one of the founding fathers of modern psychology (i.e., positive psychology). The study of positive psychology went against the norms of psychology in the day, because it didn't just bring focus to the study of those who struggled. It brought focus to the study of the successful. In Csikszentmihalyi's cornerstone research in the early stages of positive psychology, he studied the behaviours of hundreds of successfully creative people. He studied people that had had significant cultural impact. He studied scientists, artists, writers, educators, politicians, social activists, engineers, and religious leaders. What he found became largely known as 'flow' or the 'flow state'.

Flow is mastery of a skill or domain. It's a place where you lose sense of time and space as you do something truly rewarding and productive in terms of impact or output. Flow is where you are so absorbed, in creating and maintaining the conditions for that spectacularly beautiful experience, that you engage with it fully and without resistance. It's the seamless performance of dozens of dancers or the crack of a perfectly hit golf ball or the sharing of belly-aching laughter with your children. Flow is where there is perfect alignment between potential and use of a capability. It is where you fully understand the skills you have, and you fully engage them.

From a practical viewpoint, flow requires learning and practice, from both a physical and cognitive sense. You need to build the physical skills in your strength and automotive functions. You also need to get your head together, and that is much easier said than done.

If you are a golfer, or even know someone who is, you will have experienced the evasive nature of flow. Perhaps you have hit the ball well on occasions but not always. How is it that you cannot do it all the time. The answer can be found in the 1974 book by Timothy Gallwey, *The Inner Game of Tennis*. Gallwey explains that there is a gap between 'Potential' and 'Performance'. The gap is the thoughts which you have when going about an activity. In other words, the gap is interference. Gallwey's resulting formula is 'performance is equal to potential less interference'. In other words, your potential is limited by the interference, or distractions, you allow in.

We exist in a world of constant distraction. A world of 'always on'. Instant messaging can occupy our every moment. However, these external distractions aren't the biggest risk to our ability to achieve flow. It is the self-doubt, fear, and other negative emotions that hold us back. For a golfer, the test for this is simple. They just leave their phone in the club room, go onto the course alone, put earplugs in their ears and play. No matter how hard they try to remove all external distractions and interference, they'll still have their own thoughts along for the ride, getting in the way of flow.

The answer, as uncovered by Csikszentmihalyi, and other key players in positive psychology, like Martin Seligman, is to know thyself better. Specifically, you need to know your skills. You need to know what you value and your traits. It is from that place of knowledge that you build confidence and from there you keep the negative emotions at bay.

This knowledge helps you maintain control of your amygdala and bring you to a flow state more often.

Values and traits

The choices you make about where you put yourself, and what you do when you get there, are influenced by awareness of who you are.

The who that you are, is derived from core values, and personality traits. While they may shift around a little as you progress through life, fundamentally they are who you are from your teenage years, and they now drive every aspect of how you behave and respond. Values and personality traits are at the core of how you experience the world around you. As explored in chapter six, you derive beliefs from core values. You use beliefs to drive behaviours, consciously, and unconsciously. You use beliefs to evaluate your experiences, and this directly influences your sense of progress and achievement. Also, in a sense, beliefs encompass your goals in that goals represent the desired future state of something that you believe to be important. Therefore, values and personality traits are at the core of how you act and how you evaluate the experiences you have.

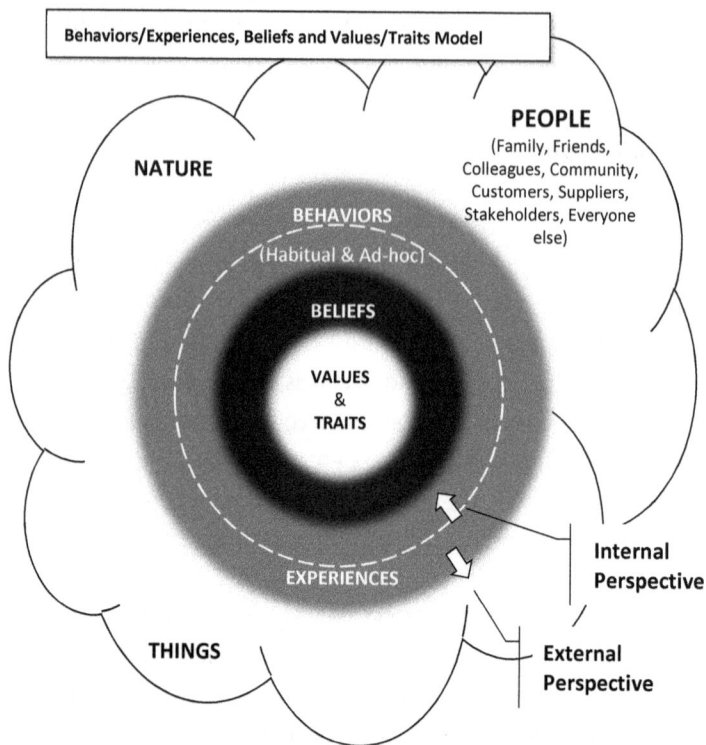

Behaviors/Experiences, Beliefs and Values/Traits Model

NATURE

PEOPLE
(Family, Friends, Colleagues, Community, Customers, Suppliers, Stakeholders, Everyone else)

BEHAVIORS
(Habitual & Ad-hoc)

BELIEFS

VALUES
&
TRAITS

EXPERIENCES

THINGS

Internal
Perspective

External
Perspective

Values are the elements of our identity that give meaning, mission, and purpose to our lives. We base our decisions on them and therefore they energize and motivate us to do things. Values are concepts like wisdom, freedom, openness, connection, personal growth, affiliation, etc. Clarifying your core values, make it easier to make decisions. Understanding core values is like learning to read the compass. A compass that has been helping you navigate through life. Interestingly, that compass isn't simplistic. Instead, we use a complex matrix, driven by context, and the level of importance. The level of importance of one value over another, affects how strongly you are motivated toward or away from a decision or experience.

With a better understanding of core values, you will be better equipped to manage your emotions and therefore respond more appropriately. More appropriate responses make it easier to build and maintain relationships.

Personality traits, or just traits, are defined as enduring patterns of perceiving, relating to, and thinking. That all relates to both our environment and how we see ourselves. In other words, they, with core values, are the building blocks of our belief system. Using 'The Big Five Aspects Scale', which is found at https://www.understandmyself.com/personality-assessment, traits with their corresponding aspects are: agreeableness, incorporating compassion and politeness; conscientiousness, incorporating industriousness and orderliness; extraversion, incorporating enthusiasm and assertiveness; neuroticism, incorporating withdrawal and volatility; and finally, openness to experience, incorporating intellect and aesthetics.

Knowing your traits is crucial to producing value. This contributes directly to a more positive state of mind. Operating within a more positive state not only helps you build better and stronger relationships, but it also helps you see opportunities.

Our understanding of traits stems from the work by Carl Jung and others in the early twentieth century. This is separate to the study of mastery of a domain of knowledge or skill, which is largely associated with Authentic Happiness, an initiative founded by Martin Seligman. Authentic Happiness is based on the idea that you excel or operate in the flow state, when you are using your skills, i.e., the desired patterns of behaviour. In Authentic Happiness these are referred to as our Signature Strengths. The idea in Authentic Happiness is that as individuals, you have varied learned or natural abilities across twenty-four Signature Strengths. Examples of these include creativity, bravery, kindness, leadership, and humour. When you engage the five or so stronger signature strengths, you are more likely to be in flow. Equally, when you are required to leverage some of the weaker signature strengths, you struggle with your energy and focus. The key, therefore, is to know your stronger signature strengths and use them as much as possible. Also, knowing where you aren't as strong is crucial, as it allows you to manage it. For example, if humour was a stronger trait and bravery wasn't, and yet you were required to enter a situation that required bravery, you could use humour before and after the situation to lift your energy and reduce the impact of having to work much harder.

While Signature Strengths are not traits, we can derive the same learning. If we know our traits, we can leverage the stronger ones to achieve flow. Equally, we can manage the weaker traits to reduce risks and depletion of energy.

Surfacing who you are

If you accept your behaviours and how you evaluate your experiences are driven by your beliefs, and you accept that this in turn is based on your values and traits, then more agency is simply a matter of uncovering your values and traits. With that awareness, you can breakdown or reinforce your beliefs. Once in full awareness of your beliefs you can directly influence the behaviours and valuations you want to engage. Coaching, be it self-coaching, or with help, allows you to build that awareness.

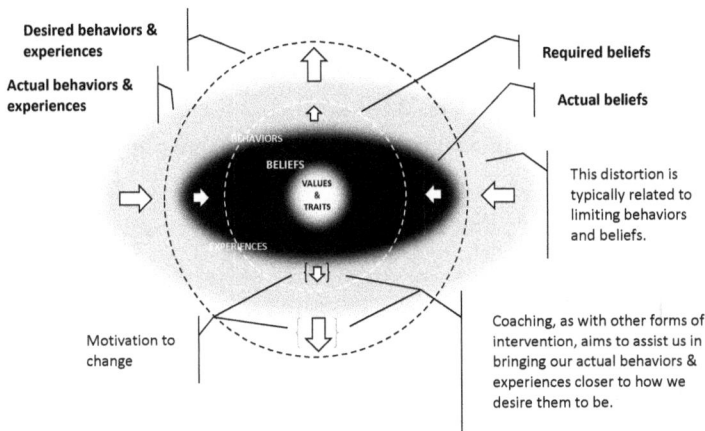

Desired behaviors & experiences

Actual behaviors & experiences

Required beliefs

Actual beliefs

BEHAVIORS

BELIEFS

VALUES & TRAITS

EXPERIENCES

This distortion is typically related to limiting behaviors and beliefs.

Motivation to change

Coaching, as with other forms of intervention, aims to assist us in bringing our actual behaviors & experiences closer to how we desire them to be.

COACHING CORNER: Building awareness of traits

Building awareness of traits can be done via psychometric tools like 'The Big Five Aspects Scale', which is found at https://www.understandmyself.com/personality-assessment.

Awareness can also be built by observing your behaviour. Like peeling layers of an onion, while straightforward, it does take effort, and time. Removing one layer of the onion allows you to get at the next layer. With each new understanding comes a new perspective.

To self-study your behaviours, you engage two parallel activities. The first activity is to spend time considering what you do well and where that is serving you. The steps for this are below. The other parallel activity is to observe your daily routines and practices and reflect on the skills you are deploying.

These questions help surface traits:

- What am I good at?
- What are my dominant gifts?
- What am I best at?
- What natural abilities do I have?
- What do I do that gets a positive response from people I respect?
- What do I do that does not seem like work, regardless of the difficulty?
- What do I do that causes doors to open with ease for me?
- What excites me?
- What activities do I enjoy the most at work, at home, or in social situations?
- What am I passionate about?
- What do I love spending time on?
- What desires keep tugging at my heart?
- What motivates me when I am most productive?
- What do I do that makes me feel good emotionally and spiritually?

Having someone else help you understand what you are good at is very efficient, but self-study and self-assessment can be just as effective.

Unlike building awareness of traits, building awareness of core values is not straightforward. It is harder because our core values are a function of our subconscious mind. Typically, we operate with beliefs that we have built around the core values, not the core values themselves. Using core values for every decision and evaluation of experiences is simply too cognitively heavy. Furthermore, these beliefs are often well established and sometimes not even our own, as discussed in chapter six. Therefore, breaking them down to surface the core values is not easy and can, at times, be a frightening experience. It is for this reason that working with a coach or therapist is the best choice. That said, there are some things that can be achieved with self-study.

To uncover your core values, without help, you can explore your experiences of decisions, and then look at what you valued during those times. The steps are as follows:

1. First, on a large piece of blank paper write a list of major decisions. Consider where you have made a difficult decision or took an unpopular course of action. Look for times when in your heart, you knew it needed to happen. Look for times when you went against the advice of those you held dear. Also look at experiences where you have made a decision, gone with it but still didn't feel right about it. List the experiences down the page.

2. Next, expand the list by considering what else drives your decisions. Consider what behaviours you find it difficult to tolerate, cause discomfort, or create stress. Look for the opposite of that behaviour and add it to your list. For example, you might get annoyed at drivers who don't let you merge into traffic. For this, write the opposite as 'Drivers allowing me to merge into traffic.'.

3. For each item listed on the page, write next to it the values that were behind the decision or that experience. Below is a list of values to help with that process. These are just a guide. Don't be afraid to come up with your own word or phrase to represent the value behind that decision or experience.

Ability	Acceptance	Accomplishment	Achievement
Acknowledgement	Action	Activity	Adaptability
Adventure	Aliveness	Aloneness	Altruism
Appearance	Approval	Art	Autonomy
Balance	Beauty	Calmness	Caring for others
Challenge	Change	Charity	Clarity
Comfort	Commitment	Communication	Community
Compassion	Competition	Complexity	Confidentiality
Connection	Consistency	Contribution	Courage
Creativity	Curiosity	Decisiveness	Difference
Dignity	Ecology	Elegance	Empathy
Entertainment	Excellence	Excitement	Exploration
Fairness	Faith	Family	Fascination
Flexibility	Forgiveness	Fortitude	Freedom
Friendship	Fulfilment	Fun	Generosity
Giving	Glory	Goals	Gratefulness
Growth	Happiness	Harmony	Health
Helpfulness	Helping	Humour	Honesty
Hope	Impact	Independence	Influence
Innovation	Integrity	Intelligence	Intimacy
Joy	Justice	Kindness	Knowledge
Laughter	Leadership	Learning	Leisure
Life	Love	Loyalty	Mastery
Meaning	Money	Music	Nature
Novelty	Openness	Order	Organization
Passion	Patience	Peacefulness	Perseverance
Personal growth	Playfulness	Pleasing others	Pleasing self
Pleasure	Positivity	Power	Privacy

Purpose	Recognition	Relationship(s)	Relaxation
Resilience	Respect	Respite	Responsibility
Rest	Safety	Security	Self-confidence
Self-discipline	Self-love	Self-reliance	Serenity
Service	Sex	Simplicity	Spirituality
Spontaneity	Sport	Stamina	Status
Staying power	Stimulating change		Stimulation
Strength	Structure	Success	Support
Survival	Teamwork	Tidiness	Tolerance
Trust	Understanding		Uniqueness
Using my abilities	Variety	Vitality	Wealth
Wisdom	Zest		

4. Next, extract the list of values onto a separate piece of paper, removing any duplicates. Write one value per line, down the left side of the page.

5. Now reflect on the values you have extracted. Give yourself time to consider what you have written. When done, get a ruler, and draw two lines down the page, to make three columns. The first column should contain your list of values. Label the second column 'Priorities' and the third column 'Honouring'.

6. Using the list of values, consider where these exist in your current situation, in terms of priority. In the middle column, give each value a number, where one represents your highest priority. Try numbering your top five first, then move into the next five, and so on. Each value must be given a unique number (i.e., you cannot have two 'priority one' values). Number them from one to the total number of values you have listed. When you are done, take time to reflect on what you see in front of you.

7. Finally, take your list of values and assess how well you are honouring that value in your life right now. Using the rightmost column, for each value, give them a number

between zero and ten. Giving a 'ten' means that you are honouring that value in EVERY decision you make and in EVERY situation at present. Giving a 'zero' means you are not honouring this value at all right now. With the 'Honouring' list you can have duplicates, i.e., you can award 'ten' to any number of your values.

To verify your self-assessment, keep it close to you over a period, perhaps over the course of the next seven days. When you make decisions, check the list. See if the value behind your decision is represented. Check to see if your priority and honouring numbering still holds true.

Finally, look at where you are not honouring high priority values. For example, scoring a five or lower in 'Honouring' against a value in the top five priorities, may represent a value that you are allowing to be squashed or put aside. It could be an indicator of a set of circumstances that you are not happy with and need to change. Consider the price you are paying for that value not being honoured, the cost to your physical and emotional wellbeing. To move forward, consider what it would take to increase the 'Honouring' number for this value.

Keeping crazy at bay

Quietening and keeping the amygdala in check is essential to staying in control and avoiding resembling a crazy person. As mentioned earlier in this chapter, to put the amygdala back to sleep, your upper brain needs to start thinking consciously about your emotions before the amygdala has found a close enough match. Once the match is found it is very hard to persuade the amygdala away from its designed purpose.

To start consciously thinking about your emotions, two conditions need to be met. The first condition is that you need to be aware of your emotions and know what to do with them. This is the concept of emotional intelligence and will be explored further in the next chapter. The other condition relates to busyness. If the emotion is particularly strong the amygdala will find a close match very quickly (i.e., in fractions of seconds). The problem here is that if your upper brain is busy, it won't be able to capture the emotion in time and start thinking about it before the amygdala does its job.

Having the ability to observe your emotions and then know what to do about them is, however, of no value if the mind is too busy thinking about other things. As David Allen suggests, we aren't talking about information overload or overwhelm, we are simply talking about an exponential increase in the rate of change. This rate of change is not matched by the skills acquired growing up (i.e., there is a gap in the skills needed to manage the complexities in life). Below are examples of where skills and complexity collide:

- Fifty instant messaging chat channels to monitor.
- Two hundred new emails appearing each day.
- A calendar of back-to-back meetings.
- An exponentially growing list of important things.
- Faces of those let down by someone turning up late.
- Needing to find new excuses for the missed commitments.

You may, or have experienced those who, subscribed to the idea that a busy mind is a good thing. This is the idea that thinking translates to active engagement and that is how stuff gets done. Unfortunately, to perform at your best, the type of thinking is also important, not just the act itself.

To perform at your best, you need to do everything you can, to keep your thinking mind clear and ready. In this state, you have the capacity to effectively process, and then respond appropriately, to everything coming at you.

As explored earlier in the chapter with the theatre metaphor, a lacking in the skills needed to manage complexity impacts performance, and that affects productivity. The evidence of this is in the existence of the Amygdala Hijack. All we need to do is measure, in ourselves and those around us, the frequency at which the Amygdala Hijack occurs. Unless we are talking about life-threatening situations, an Amygdala Hijack is a good indicator that the mind has been too busy to efficiently process an emotion. Every time an Amygdala Hijack occurs there is a strong possibility that someone isn't being rational or isn't performing with full awareness of the specific situation. The resulting decisions are often inappropriate and create more work in undoing damage. That extra work impacts productivity. It is where days appear to roll into one another with seemingly little forward momentum.

In chapter twenty, we will explore how to leverage the awareness of what you do well and what you value, to reduce the craziness you experience.

Chapter 14: Because you care

Agency embraces emotions.

Unlocking the potential of emotions

Emotions are indicators of something in our experience of the world that we should move closer to or further away from. The strength of the emotion gives the level of importance in our mind and the speed at which we should move.

When we think of emotions, there will be a few big-ticket names that always get a mention, like love, hate, and fear. However, while there are ways of categorizing and grouping them, they all play in our minds, and both enable and hinder our journey. To make things a little easier, lets focus on the two sides of the same coin (i.e., negative and positive emotions).

Examples of negative emotions include fear, disgust, boredom, hate, envy, sorrow, anger, frustration, annoyance, discontentment, alarm, anxiety, guilt, and indifference.

Examples of positive emotions include joy, love, happiness, gratitude, serenity, interest, hope, amusement, inspiration, awe, elevation (from acts of kindness), altruism (from selfless giving), satisfaction, relief, affection, cheerfulness, surprise (good), confidence (self-efficacy), admiration, enthusiasm, eagerness, euphoria, peacefulness, and optimism.

Emotions are the basis of our freeze, flight, or fight response managed by the amygdala, as explored in chapter thirteen. Equally, they are a key input to our managed thinking in the human part of our brain. Emotions both keep us safe and put us in danger. They hold us back from engaging fully and helping others. Emotions drive selfless giving and sacrifice. They enable us to engage passionately with a specific subject or experience. Emotions are the fuel that brings us toward and through our challenges. They are the glue that brings us into and out of connection and bonds with our fellow human beings.

Skill in being aware of emotions and knowing what to do with them (i.e., emotional intelligence), is crucial to success in having a better experience of the world. At the heart of this skill in observing emotions in ourselves and others, is the ability to observe our thinking as we experience the world, as explored in chapter thirteen. Being conscious of your thoughts and actions is important because it allows you to engage your thinking brain, and once you do that you are in control. Once the prefrontal cortex is engaged, you need to know what to do with those emotions. Key to that is your understanding of what you value and your traits. It is important to have this understanding, so that when something comes before you, you have a better than average chance of knowing what to do with it.

Catching emotions and Caring

COACHING CORNER: Managing emotions.

Emotional intelligence can be taught and improved with practice. A good place to start is labelling, also known as naming emotions. This is the technique of using your self-talk to your advantage, and there isn't much to it. You simply use a phrase like 'I am experiencing excitement' or 'I am experiencing fear' or 'I am experiencing anger.' Saying it quietly in your head is enough. Saying it out loud can help also, particularly if that emotion is strong. The technique is enhanced by repeating it over and over, until you feel a sense of calm and control returning. Once that sense of calm and control returns, your thinking brain is back in the driver's seat. Once you are in that place, you can look at the emotion and its meaning. Clearly, none of this works if you can't observe the emotion in the first place. Practice is the key to that. It is best to start small and build up.

To build the skill, you start with naming emotions in normal situations, like joy, and contentment. You name these in your mind. From there you observe how the mind reacts to thinking about them. While it may feel hard at first, it gets easier with practice. This practice is explored further as part of building the attention muscle at the end of chapter eighteen.

An effective way to manage strong emotions is to tell yourself that they are with you because you care.

When you are feeling nervous, consider that this is because the challenge at hand is important to you. When you are feeling scared, consider that perhaps you don't want to let yourself or others down. When you are feeling angry, consider that it might be that your expectations haven't been met. When you feel love, consider that you are engaged in something of meaning. When you feel excited, consider that you are engaging in something that is important to you.

When an emotion captures your attention, ask yourself, 'So what?'. Explore what level of importance you are associating with the thoughts that follow that question. Look for the level of 'care' you have for those thoughts. It is through this self-talk that emotions get managed.

Fighting the right cause

Negative emotions, like anger and frustration, are both a powerful friend and foe in the fight against the behaviours that hold you back. Giving into and avoiding truths about your own mental state is both a cause of harm and loss of learning opportunity. Unfortunately, the cards are stacked against us. Some struggle to deal with negative emotions properly because few want to acknowledge their own disappointment. People often prefer to say nothing and keep working. They look for distractions to hide the pain (i.e., engage in substance abuse, obsessive sports, volunteering etc). This is done instead of truly facing the negative emotions. When you allow yourself to experience the emotions properly, you can use them to drive your energy. You can use this awareness to bring focus to the changes you need to make to yourself and the context you operate within. You can also use these emotions to fight.

Fighting is an important aspect of our survival. Among other things, it helps us stand up for ourselves, a skill that has helped us over the ages achieve many things. As well as defending what we have, fighting has helped our ancestors get fed and win that prized spouse so we can procreate. Fighting does not come without its problems, specifically in the modern world when the response is invoked because of the Amygdala Hijack. Just being in control of your negative emotions isn't enough to function productively. As with all emotions, you need to channel the associated energy somewhere appropriate. For example, take the idea of using a punching bag. Even two minutes of pounding the bag brings a whole new focus to your energy. Others do Rocky Balboa style air-punching during exercise. When you control your negative emotions, you bring the focus back to something you can use. You can use it to fight the right cause.

To understand negative emotions, as with all your emotions, you simply need to bring them to your conscious mind and then explore what they mean to you. This process is greatly aided by talking with a supportive friend, being coached, and using counselling/psychotherapy. Acknowledgment of the negative emotion is the first step. Once in that awareness, you must own it and experience it. From there you can shake it off and drive forward. You can help yourself by looking for the opposite and what it would take to reach that place. From the dark you come back into the light.

Negative emotions, when explored properly, serve three purposes. Firstly, they are an excellent motivator in that they give you something to fight for. Secondly, in exploring the negative emotions, you uncover the limiting or borrowed beliefs as explored in part one. That awareness enables you to engage agency. And finally, mastery in managing your own emotions is going to make it much easier to help others manage theirs, especially those you care about.

Managing derailing behaviours

Knowing only positive experiences, engaging only with loving, and caring people and having everything always where it needs to be, is the stuff of fairy tales. Life just isn't like that. Life is full of negativity and negative experiences.

Furthermore, negativity around you, also creates the near perfect conditions for the Amygdala Hijack. However, how you engage with the crappy side of life is a choice.

Removing yourself from negative circumstances and distancing yourself from people who invoke strong emotions, is lovely in theory. Sure, you could change jobs, leave the gym, move to a different city or stop spending time with a negative friend. However, you won't and can't remove the potential entirely. You will always have to endure potentially derailing behaviour from friends, family members, colleagues, those in your communities, or important business contacts.

Angry, miserable people want us to be drawn into their misery so that they feel less alone with it. Left unmanaged it is potentially catastrophic. From the body of work pioneered by Vilayanur Ramachandran, we have learnt that we mirror the emotions of others. You may find that when you don't protect your own positive state, you can easily get caught up in everything about their problems and start compromising on who you are.

COACHING CORNER: Managing derailing behaviours.

There are three potential strategies for managing derailing behaviours from those you care about or must deal with for professional reasons:

1. Confronting: This strategy involves telling them straight and giving them direct feedback. However, confronting is only worthwhile if the other party is in a place of seeing growth as a possibility. If they aren't ready to learn and forgive themselves, the confronting approach won't help. In certain situations, confronting can even cause more harm and make things more challenging. For example, standing up to a skilled bully can have you looking like the aggressor and have the bully looking like the victim. This doesn't serve anyone.

2. Ignoring: This strategy is as the title suggests. Turning away and ignoring those who are behaving badly helps in the short term. However, by ignoring them, you are buying into their misery. That may cause more hurt for you than dealing with the hurt caused by the misery they inflict.

3. Disarming: In his book Talking to Crazy: How to Deal with the Irrational and Impossible People in Your Life, Mark Goulston

explores various forms of irrational behaviour. As well as helping to understand the irrational behaviour, he provides details on how to manage ourselves in these situations. Goulston also shares ideas on how we can help the other person get to a better place. For example, Goulston's insights provide a method to counteract negative behaviour. He suggests that you try to be over-the-top with positivity and you do it constantly and deliberately. As often as you can, you start by asking the person how they are. Or in a professional context, you ask, 'How are things going for you?' You do it in a positive and cheerful manner. Then when they reply with the usual, 'I am tired', 'I am not well', 'I have got loads to do', or whatever it is, you empathise (i.e., you say, 'That must be terrible for you', or something like that). You then change the subject to something positive, and perhaps unrelated to the concern expressed (i.e., when hearing about a poor grade in math, you might say 'It is great that Johnny got eighty percent in his spelling test'). Another example could be on hearing about 'being really busy', you could say, 'It is great that the company closed that deal with xyz the other day'. Even if the other person doesn't hear or take in what you are saying, by using this approach you maintain your positive state of mind. You may also feel that you are there for the other person when they are ready to move forward.

When you encounter someone exhibiting derailing behaviour that you cannot just remove from your life, like a family member, colleague, or important work contact, you need to do what you can to help, but not at the risk of compromising yourself. Whether the person is just going through a bad patch or has some clinical issues, while useful at times, confronting or ignoring only makes things worse for you, and them. Disarming, using techniques like deliberate positivity, on the other hand, helps you maintain your own positive state and may even help them with theirs.

Gratefulness

A useful trick when it comes to emotions and the mysterious workings of the mind is presented beautifully by Goulston. He suggests that it is impossible to feel gratitude and anger at the same time. Moving yourself to a positive and more constructive place on a regular basis is key to agency. You can reduce anger and other negative emotions simply by being grateful. Additionally, engagement of the gratefulness emotion may even give you a good boost when you are already in a positive place.

Various research studies and books have explored the benefits of gratitude (i.e., Seligman, Steen, Park & Peterson (2005), and Sheldon & Lyubomirsky (2006)). A common theme is the use of a daily reflection of three things to be grateful for. A good place to start is to first explore these techniques with the three-week challenge.

COACHING CORNER: Three-week gratefulness challenge.

The three-week gratefulness challenge involves a daily capture of three things that you are grateful for. The process involves a daily reminder in your calendar, and a place to write. The process involves writing 'I am grateful for ...' or 'I am grateful that I am ...'. You write three of these sentences daily for twenty-one days. It can be different things or the same. It doesn't matter too much. The impact on your state of mind should be noticeable. During the twenty-one days and for several weeks after, you should feel better about yourself and more able to face your daily challenges. If unsure of the benefits, repeat the process about six months later and see what happens. Many adopt this practice as a daily ritual. It is especially useful during times of trouble and stress. The ritual may even help as you drive into the unknown.

We will explore more uses of gratitude in chapter twenty-one.

Chapter 15: Give and take

Agency is more than a solo act.

With others, is more fun

While not always a positive experience, time with others is certainly a rich environment for learning and growing. Furthermore, your experience of life is greatly enhanced when you give help, advice and pleasure to others, and vice versa. However, there are risks associated with how and how much you give or receive. Too much or too little in either direction can decrease your experience of life and increase your chances of finding yourself alone.

Adam Grant in his 2014 book *Give and Take: Why Helping Others Drives Our Success*, presents case studies and research to show that the majority of those who have had the most success in life, across a range of measures, are givers. Takers don't always make the top of the list as one might expect. Matchers exist in the middle, and there is no surprise there. The startling thing is that while those that give are at the top, they also exist at the bottom. Those that give too much, unconditionally, get taken advantage of and marginalized. Only those that give in a way that stays true to themselves in an uncompromising way, succeed. This alternative approach to giving is what Grant calls 'Otherish Giving'. It is the idea that you give where it works both for yourself and others. It's a win-win. It's not the same as matching, which is giving something, and expecting something back of equal or similar quality and quantity. Otherish Giving is unconditional giving, but it's done in a way which allows you to still build and maintain your own physical, mental, and financial wellbeing. It holds true to the notion that to help others we must help ourselves first. We must take that oxygen mask and use it before assisting others. We must take that help or advice when it is offered and use it gratefully without carrying guilt or a feeling of owing. And we must give back unconditionally but in measures that don't compromise our own wellbeing.

It is in the social needs

Your social needs are complex, as are the social needs of those in your life. You need lots of different things. As do those you care about and associate with. You need others to be interested in what you are doing (i.e., to listen, to empathise with, and to guide you). You need to be needed (i.e., you need to have opportunities to listen to, to empathise with, and to guide). You need someone to call you out when you are putting yourself down, being unrealistic, or simply aiming too high. You need others to care for and to provide for. You need to feel that you are helping in ways that are needed. These needs stretch across a spectrum from intimate/physical, to spiritual, social, and professional. You have physical needs, from the intimate sexual, to hugs with loved ones, to sharing the same physical proximity in social and professional settings. You need to share joy and humour in various forms, from the family-friendly to edgy and adult only. You need to share challenges. You need to share pain and anguish. You need to share excitement and wonder. And you need to share worthiness.

Unfortunately, all your needs can't be satisfied by any single individual. There are just too many and they are too complex. Equally, it's downright limiting to believe that the good that you can bring to the world can be achieved through a couple of associations. Your needs are complicated and varied, and so too is the network of associations required to meet those needs. Relying on a single person for all your needs is an awful burden to place on them, especially someone you care about.

You need all kinds of different people in your life if you are truly going to be able to satisfy your social needs. You need dependents, confidants, adversaries, champions, challengers, givers, takers, followers, and role models. You need different things from different people. Those people need different things from you. And what you give to any individual may not necessarily be reciprocated. You may have a friend that often calls for your support, but never offers support back. The mistake here is to see that as wrong. It simply is not. It is unrealistic to expect that everyone in your life is in the same place as you are at any given moment. An individual relationship may change over time and balance out, but it may not either.

Who will fix your car tire?

Understanding what you need is challenging. Understanding if you are truly having those needs met is a whole different sort of challenge.

Consider the challenge of needing help with a slightly deflated car tire. Being slightly deflated might mean you don't notice it— you might be happily driving around the place unaware that you are putting stress on the tire and increasing the possibility of a more serious problem, like a blow-out. Now consider if someone else notices the deflated car tire. They have a quandary. Do they tell you about it or just ignore it? If they tell you about it, they risk certain things. They risk injuring your ego and being shot down for delivering the message. That might bring them unwanted stress. Alternatively, you might love the drama and invite them to help you fix it. That might get in the way of their plans. If you ask for help, what might that help be? Let's assume you asked for help, either because of someone telling you or because of you noticing the problem yourself. Consider what the possible response might be. Perhaps the other person might offer to use their pump. Perhaps they might even offer to take the car and get it sorted for you. Perhaps the other person might simply give directions to the nearest place to get the tire inflated. Perhaps the person might take an easier option for them, and simply suggest you abandon the possibility of reflating the tire and suggest you replace it, either with the spare, or by getting someone else to do it. The different types of responses will indicate the different levels of interest in you and your immediate challenge. Now consider if this challenge wasn't a slightly deflated tire. What if the challenge was an unfaithful spouse, or a child seen doing something they shouldn't, or a friend speaking behind your back, or a failing business venture, or an unfulfilling job? How would those in your network respond? Would they tell you? What level of support would they give you? Would they help find a solution or would they take an easier path, and suggest you walk away from the challenge?

In understanding how you get your social needs met, you need to avoid having 'car insurance companies' in the mix. Not all those in your network have your best interests at heart. You may need them to satisfy your own needs, (i.e., you support them). However, expecting them to reciprocate might bring you more pain. Car insurance companies extract premiums with the promise of support. When something goes wrong, they come to the rescue. However, there is often an excess payment needed before that help comes. Worse still is that when the damage is significant and the possible path to resolution long and hard, they are far too willing to write it off completely. They will offer compensation that is based on the market and often far less than the utility value. Even with cars, this is often unsatisfactory. Consider if the challenge wasn't your car, but your marriage, your parenting, business, or career. Having someone in your network suggest that you simply write it off is inadequate and may lead to larger problems.

Groups need people

It sounds obvious, but we often forget the fact that a group needs people. We need more than two people for things to work in a social or professional setting involving a group of people sharing, experiencing, or working together. Have you ever found yourself needing to justify your involvement in any group setting. Perhaps you appreciate, that when it is just you and someone else it is clear there is going to be some give and perhaps take, and that both of you have a role. However, for groups of three or more, did you feel you needed a reason to be there. Did you feel that you needed to have some clear contribution to make or some skill to bring. That might not be the case because groups need people (i.e., to share ideas or concerns, we need an audience). So, simply being present in the group, at times, might be enough. The right number of people in a group setting increases the value for all involved, even if it's simply just to listen.

While passive involvement in a group setting does work at times, it's not always optimal. When it comes to teams, the interdependency of skills and tasks require active engagement from all those involved.

When you show up and get involved, be it to share or listen, you create wonderful opportunities for growth, both in yourself, and others.

That one special person

The burden of choice has the potential to be particularly heavy when it comes to that one person that means the world to you.

For most, love is a confusing concept. You may have experienced love in different forms, as a son/daughter, sibling, grandson/granddaughter, nephew/niece, cousin, friend, lover, spouse, father/mother, colleague, team member, or leader. And hopefully, you've had opportunities to love. However, is being loved or sharing love, the same as being 'in love'? Or is there a difference between loving something about another or simply 'loving' them. And more importantly, does it really matter? Is 'in love' really about infatuation? Does it simply fuel the honeymoon stage of a relationship? Also, is 'loving someone' simply about caring unconditionally?

Does 'in love' automatically translate to being loved or being able to love? Is not to be loved or to love context specific. Does it need to be all-encompassing. Sure, you need high levels of trust for love to work properly, however that trust only needs to extend as far as the context requires it. For example, being loved by a parent requires a level of trust that is not the same as being loved by a lover. The types of honesty required in those situations isn't the same.

Love is just another need, be it a quite complicated one. How you achieve love depends on the context and that can vary. It is a mistake to believe all your love needs can be obtained from one individual. Holding onto this belief gets in the way of building strong relationships or getting out of bad ones. That isn't to say that you must satisfy the same need via multiple different people. While you can get the same type of love you need as a son/daughter from both parents, or as a brother/sister from multiple siblings or a leader from thousands of followers, there are certain types of love, specifically the intimate kind, which might be best sourced from a single individual. The trick is to narrow down the specific needs from each person in your life and not overly burden one individual with more than is reasonable to expect of them.

Trust

Trust is crucial to relationships. Behaviours that build trust include a one hundred percent commitment to sharing feelings, both positive, and negative. Behaviours that build trust include acknowledging your desires (i.e., talking openly about what you need, what isn't being met, and being honest when you are attracted to, or aroused by, someone outside the relationship). Having desires that aren't agreeable within the relationship or being attracted to someone else doesn't automatically lead to infidelity, or even the demise of the relationship. You are kidding yourself if you claim you have never been attracted to or been aroused by someone else while already in a relationship. It's the lack of honesty that causes grief. Instead of being honest with your spouse, you may feel guilt. You may feel you have done something wrong, simply because your natural desires were aroused by someone else. Getting berated by your spouse for sharing your desires, no matter where they come from, isn't about you, it's about them. It is a signal that they have baggage, be it a self-image problem or some deeper psychological issues. It is totally unrealistic and a perfect reason to visit some hard questions about the nature of the relationship. Behaviours that build trust include being honest about all the aspects, including what excites you, what scares you, and what's in the way. Behaviours that build trust include assuming the right intent, always.

Building trust and therefore the ability to love, starts with trust. That sounds like a chicken and egg conversation, and that's because it is. Trust doesn't start with distrust. Trust starts with trust. Starting from a position of trust requires courage and, fundamentally, belief in yourself. For example, and as touched on in chapter thirteen, think about the last time you said or heard 'What are you thinking?'. For the person asking the question, why did they ask that question? Is something worrying them about the other person? Did the other person do or say something that confuses them? Does the way they look imply that something needs to be talked about? Or is the person doing the asking really trying to distract themselves from their own thoughts? Perhaps the person doing the asking is hiding something and doesn't want to talk about it. Perhaps the person doing the asking is just bored and doesn't want to own up to that. What about the person being asked? What happens to them when they receive this question? When you try to second guess what another is feeling or thinking, you invite suspicion. When you share that you are worried or scared, you invite trust.

Growing together (or not)

Relationships are not straightforward, intimate ones being the most complex. As already explored in chapter three, traction in starting relationships is aided by dropping the barriers and then allowing yourself to explore what you could do better. From that place you can learn and grow. It is that aspect that allows the strongest bonds to be built. Learning and growing together creates shared experiences. These shared experiences can be joyous but also painful. Either way they are shared, and that can have its advantages. Looking back at yourself and laughing, or crying, is the fuel that helps you move through and beyond the daily grind. And, doing that with someone who shares those lessons, or at least can relate to them, is nothing short of magical. It is for this reason that you might consider choosing carefully when building trust with new people. You really should not be bothered engaging with someone that doesn't want to see their experiences as opportunities for learning. You should give a wide birth to anyone that claims they have all the answers or no problems. Everyone has baggage and things to learn. For those who accept they don't have their stuff together, they are lucky, because through acceptance, they are already eighty percent there. They are on their way to getting their stuff together. It is those that are in denial that really need attention. These people will find themselves without a spear and face-to-face with a vicious carnivore, or in the path of a fast-moving bus. You wouldn't want to be anywhere near them when it all goes horribly wrong.

They say, 'A problem shared is a problem halved.'. This is all well and good in theory. Consider, if one person was the single recipient of the 'halves', for all your problems or even worse, for everyone they know.

Those 'halves' would soon add up to a lot of 'wholes'. That's too much for anyone to shoulder. Coming home after a hard day and offloading the day's challenges on your spouse is easy and gives you relief. But at what cost? If you did that day after day, things aren't going to end well! The weight of the difficult stuff you endure is better shared around. Perhaps there are some aspects of your challenging experiences that can be shared with a colleague or friend, before you get home. Spreading the burden of your woes, has the same benefit for your own mental wellbeing, and it reduces the load on that someone special in your life. The same goes for individual friends or family members. You don't want to be bottling up all your worries and concerns and carrying them around with you only to then dump them on family members when you find yourself with them. Sharing all your baggage in one big offload is too much for anyone to endure.

Helping others will help you in many ways. Least of all it will help you build your own skill in observing and managing your emotions. However, helping others is not straightforward. This is especially challenging when the ego is driving your thinking (more on that topic in chapter twenty-one).

If you feel someone near you needs help, the best thing to do is to ask them. You might simply say to them 'Are you okay?' When you get a 'no', you then simply ask them how you may help them and do it in a manner that makes this about them and not you. For example, instead of saying, 'Oh, I am sorry to hear that, how may I help you?' you might say, 'Oh, I am sorry to hear that. What would help you right now?' This latter suggestion makes it about them, not you. You then need to be open to what comes back and be prepared to go out of your way to help. If what they ask of you is something that compromises who you are, you need to tell them exactly that. For example, you might respond with 'I don't feel comfortable doing that; it doesn't agree with what I feel is right for me.' Silence is also very useful here as it might help them rationalize the situation and suggest something else. Doing anything other than what is asked for, even if you feel it is in their interest, is your values and beliefs speaking, not theirs. That also applies to suggesting something they did not ask for. It's likely just going to annoy them and push them away.

On the other hand, if you get a 'Yes, everything is okay' to your initial question, and you feel that isn't the case, you could try to give them space. The amount of space will be very specific to the situation—it could be minutes, hours, days, weeks, or even months. However, you may not like to turn away if you have strong concerns. An alternative could be to approach someone that also knows this person and let them know you are concerned. When sharing with another, you shouldn't elaborate too much as it risks bringing your judgment into the situation. That could be counterproductive. You might simply say, 'I have a feeling ___ isn't okay.', and leave it at just 'a feeling.'. You might just leave it here and not even suggest any action but leave that to the other person to initiate.

Not all relationships will serve you. There are big advantages in being there to help others, as there is in allowing others to help you. You need to give to receive. And you need to give others the opportunity to do the same. However, there is a difference between someone genuinely needing help and someone simply being needy. When you find yourself the constant recipient of offloading with little opportunity for your own personal growth, you need to be honest with yourself. It is hard to say no when someone is in need. It is hard to say, 'no, actually my needs come first.'. Unfortunately, you must have courage. That hard choice is in your best interest, as well as theirs. Toxic people and their behaviours have no place in your life. They can devastate your experience and wellbeing. For example, there is no place for someone who says something toxic quietly to make you angry, then says something trivial and unrelated out loud to attract attention, thus giving the impression that you are angry and unreasonable to anyone else in the room. There is no place for behaviours involving manipulation, seeking admiration and special treatment, or that are callous and insensitive. Choosing who you learn and grow with, takes investment and vigilance. To ensure you have productive relationships, you must be flexible, but also willing to change who you invite into your life.

The investment

There is an extension to the doorstep concept that we explored in chapter seven. The idea is that once you get over the need to present a rose-coloured view of yourself, you start to let people in. The 'Door' (or hall), 'Lounge' and 'Kitchen' work well to explain the stages you go through. So, let's picture someone calling to your door. If you don't know or trust them, you are unlikely to let them over the doorstep. Depending on your home configuration and the weather, you may let them into the hall, but only just, and with the door left open. The conversation happens and ends there. Now, consider they call again. Perhaps you now know more about them. Perhaps you asked around and have some level of respect for them or you like them. But you don't trust them yet. So, now you bring them into the lounge, or 'Good Room'. You might offer them coffee, tea, biscuits, and cake. This space is somewhat staged and presents your best self. You keep this space tidy, and it doesn't give too much away about the way you live and who you are. The conversations now take a slightly richer colour but are not fully open. Let's move forward. So, you've enjoyed multiple conversations in the lounge and the trust has built up to a good level. This is the point they get invited to sit at the kitchen table. From the kitchen table they get to see the real you. They get to see the disarray, the worn surfaces, and chipped cups. They get to see how you live your life and who you are. It is not realistic that everyone you know will sit at your kitchen table, nor do you want that. There are plenty of associations that will work perfectly from the doorstep. There are many that will serve your and their needs, simply in the lounge. However, to build the network of associations that will meet your social needs, you must let the right people sit at your kitchen table. That will take time and effort to know who is truly worthy.

All good things take investment and ongoing maintenance. Building meaningful and purposeful social, intimate, and professional relationships is no different. The effort needed should not be overlooked or taken for granted. It's unrealistic to think it will just happen. It takes effort, and not just upfront. It takes effort over the course of the relationship. It's not like winning the lotto (i.e., a small investment with big returns), which is fun to play but takes little or no effort. Things get tough over the course of a relationship. The storms that you face will put pressure into places you don't expect: the economic downturns, personal injury or ill-health, the sudden illness or death of loved ones, and other changes around you. It is unrealistic to expect not to see these in your journey. If you have under-invested, it is during these tough times that the cracks will widen and you risk sinking. Equally, too much focus on the long-term play is just as limiting. You are going to struggle to have an engaging experience if you only put a penny in each month. Very little will come of that until perhaps when you are in your seventies, retired, looking at buying a new outfit for your neighbour's funeral. It might work for superficial 'Doorstep' acquaintances, but not for rewarding long-term 'kitchen table' relationships. Life is to be lived today, not tomorrow. You need to invest big at the offset and be willing to continue to put more in over the course of time.

The Social Needs Relationship Matrix

Reward is not without risk. It's an old saying and it is so true, and it applies to investing the time and effort in building relationships to meet your social needs. It is hard at the start of a new association to be completely open. Perhaps you fear that you will be taken advantage of or hurt. Perhaps you fear the effort will be wasted if things don't go the distance. Those fears will hold you back. You may carry fears of one-nightstands or getting to know the new neighbour, part-time or casual labour colleagues because there's no guarantee you will be seeing or working with them again tomorrow. However, there is a middle ground. The middle ground is being clear about who you are, being realistically optimistic, being clear about what you need, and allowing yourself to give and to receive. We will explore more of bringing all that together in chapter nineteen, for now let's focus on the social needs and build from there.

COACHING CORNER: *Social Needs Relationship Matrix.*

The Social Needs Relationship Matrix is used to assess whether your social needs are being met by those in your world. This tool helps you see where you need to focus effort, both from an initial investment, and, from a maintenance viewpoint. It gives a clear line of sight. The steps are as follows:

1. Open a spreadsheet or use a piece of graph paper.

2. In the first column, down the page, list your social needs, putting one need per row.

In exploring your social needs, look at what you need in terms of giving and receiving. Also look at aspects of your personal and professional experience. If you get stuck, think about the interactions you have had with others. Consider what topics were part of those interactions. Consider who was doing the talking and who was doing the listening. Look for experiences with others where you felt high levels of emotions, both positive and negative. Describe the opportunities for giving and receiving separately. be very specific when you know there is an interaction that you need from one individual and be more general when a group of people are involved.

Here are some examples:

Support me in my physical wellbeing
Support others in their physical wellbeing
Support me in building better habits
Support others in building better habits
Listen to/empathise with my ideas of intimacy
Guide me in my ideas of intimacy
Listen to/empathise with my ideas on building friendship
Guide me in my ideas of building friendships
Listen to/empathise with my personal development ideas
Guide me in my personal development
Listen to/empathise with my professional development ideas
Guide me in my professional development
Listen to/empathise with my spirituality related notions
Guide me in my spirituality
Listen to/empathise with other's ideas of intimacy
Guide others in their ideas of intimacy
Listen to/empathise with others in their personal endeavours
Guide others in their personal endeavours
Listen to/empathise with others in their professional endeavours
Guide others in their professional endeavours
Sexual Intimacy
Hugs
Play
Physical proximity
Call me out for putting myself down.
Call me out for being unrealistic/aiming too high.
Care for/provide for
Share joy/humour—family
Share joy/humour—adult
Share value creation
Share growing (pain/anguish)
Share excitement/wonder

Share worthiness

3. In each of the column headings, write the name of key people or groups of people in your life. For example, write the name of your girlfriend/boyfriend/spouse in column two, the names of each of your children in the next columns, the names of your parents and siblings in the next set of columns, key extended family members after that, and then your business partners, followed by the names of your close friends. Then put key clients, key influencers and your various groups, communities, and professional associations in separate column headings after that. And, finally, list your support network (i.e., your doctor, coach, trainer etc).

4. Now review each cell and give it a number, if appropriate. Either leave it blank, or give it a one, two, or three. Leave the cell blank if that person or group of people has no impact whatsoever on the social need. Give the cell a one or a two if the person or group occasionally helps meet that social need. Give one if there is a good bit of effort required on your part (i.e., if you must go out of your way to bring this person into your life to help with the related social need), otherwise give a two. Give a three when that person regularly helps you with that social need.

The results would look something like the following:

Need	Spouse	Son 1	Son 2	Colleague	Client	Doctor
Support me in my physical wellbeing	2					1
Hugs	3	2	2		1	
Listen to / Empathize with my professional development ideas	1			1		
Guide others in their professional endeavors	1			1	3	

5. With the scores in place, add them up, and look for patterns. Consider that there is a need for investment when, across your existing connections, you are not getting at least three in total (i.e., in the example above 'Listen to/empathise with my professional development ideas' isn't being met). Perhaps you need to take action to address that. Secondly, look for big winners (i.e., 'Spouse' in this example has the highest score). If you are to maintain the current level of wellbeing, you had better invest effort to make sure that relationship is well-maintained.

To work on the patterns, perhaps print or copy the work. Then write your action plan directly against the needs and individuals you want to focus on. Later, you can revisit that piece of paper to reflect on your progress.

The patterns you see in this chart will be relevant for where you are now. Over time, these will shift as you change, and as people come into and out of your life. Perhaps revisit this matrix as you need to (i.e., when you meet new people, lose contact, or something major shifts in an existing relationship).

The matrix provides useful information in helping you manage your network of friends, family, and peers. It will show you where you need to invest and maintain. It will also show you where you have risks. It is worth considering action if you see a single individual scoring two or three times higher than anyone else. Not only does it show that the individual has a lot to shoulder, but it shows you to be in a vulnerable position should that individual no longer be part of your life. That could be because of a breakup or falling out. It could simply be because you change your context, and they aren't as available anymore. It could also be because of something more painful, like death, or someone becoming mentally incapacitated. The pain and ability to bounce forward after a significant loss is going to be considerably more difficult if that departed individual was also a key part of your support network. There is a lot of merit in widening your network through rekindling old friendships and repairing bridges, especially as you get older. Clearly, it isn't realistic to suggest that you shouldn't have anyone in your life that you rely on and will miss dearly. You should just be mindful of how much you focus on one individual and have some alternatives available. It is simply important to have the support around you when you need it.

Chapter 16: Bringing your body with you

Agency involves action.

Fitness

There is nothing straightforward to keeping in shape and maintaining adequate energy levels, especially when you are fast approaching, or beyond, mid-life. Things start to creak, get wobbly, greyer, and less responsive. Even those who in their earlier years could eat what they like, do very little exercise, and still bounce through their day with vigour and enthusiasm, will eventually find themselves lethargic, inflexible and being a whole lot more buoyant than they'd like. And, at all ages, busyness can drain your mental energy by late afternoon.

Furthermore, a poor self-image, be it based on fact or fiction, will impact how you behave. It can influence your attitude to exercise, food, drink and sleep. Inappropriate attention to any of that also affects your cognitive potential.

Right fit

Holding a borrowed belief, about what type of exercise suits you, is not a good look. Getting stuck on what we can and can't do with respect to exercise is like all things relating to a fixed mindset, it has the potential to hold you back.

However, getting into the right form of exercise for you, doesn't typically happen overnight; it takes focus and time. It must be realistic, and it also requires motivation. We will return to motivation later in the chapter.

Fuel and poison

For many, food and drink are seen as rewards. It makes sense really if you think back to the hunter-gatherer times, when it took days of effort to kill or collect even a modest meal. Food is also seen as comforting. Which also makes sense if you consider in the past, we may have gone days without seeing a morsel. There is no wonder, therefore, as to why you may reach for a snack, when you are feeling both disappointed and excited. You could even say that it is our nature.

In modernity this 'nature' can be counterproductive. Making decisions, about what food or drink to take on, when stressed or tired, is never a good idea. Those poor decisions often compound the problem because we don't get what we really need.

Let's be very honest, there is no magic wand on this. There is no straightforward set of steps. No one solution that works unilaterally. However, awareness and attention to some of the detail does help.

Another thing that might help is doing what you can do to reverse the belief that 'food and drink is reward'. A better belief might be that food and drink are the fuel to obtain reward. Consider how different things would be if you chose to eat and drink because you needed to, but not as the reward for using energy. This alternative belief might even help you feel better about yourself.

Recovery

Sleep is important. It is a myth that 'there will be plenty of time for sleep when you are six feet under, pushing up daisies.' Equally, it is counterproductive to believe that in order to get more done and engage with life better, you need to be awake more. Finally, it serves you little to believe that sleep is for amateurs—for lazy people who don't amount to much.

Even if you love the idea of sleep, if that sleep isn't of sufficient quality, things will be harder than they should be. Relishing the softness of the bed and the feeling of pulling up the duvet after a long and busy day, if you then toss and turn, or wake up loads, does not give your body what it needs.

The benefits of quality sleep are widely understood. It is also clear that sleep is necessary for the brain to repair. Thinking involves acetylcholine, glutamate, and dopamine along with neurotransmitters being released from one neuron into the synapse (the tiny gaps between neurons). For simplicity's sake, let's call all of that 'brain fuel'. While we can replenish our supply of brain fuel, often the replenishing can't keep up, particularly if what we are doing is cognitively heavy. It only catches up when we rest our mind properly, like when we are in deep sleep. If we do not give our brain time to recover, we stop being able to make decisions effectively. It is a bit like playing a graphics intensive game on your phone with the charger plugged in. The charger cannot keep up with the power needs of the game, so even with the power plug connected, eventually the phone battery depletes to nothing.

A near certain way to experience the depletion of brain fuel is to fly between London and Sydney and drink and watch movies the whole way. On the ground, and after the excitement of seeing old friends and family wears off, things get wobbly. As the fatigue takes over, you go through stages of annoyance, then anger, and then confusion. At some point after that, you will get completely zombie-like. You won't be able to think, and your body will simply stop functioning. New parents experience a similar temporary degradation of cognitive function. Another way to think of this is like dirty dishes. If you simply stack the dishes and keep making new meals without washing up, eventually there will be either no dishes to use or no space to cook, or both. The kitchen becomes unusable.

There are many ways to improve the quality of sleep. Here is a list of some of these:

- Regular bedtime (within wriggle room of fifteen to twenty minutes either end) directly impacts life longevity and cognitive fitness.
- Improving sleep requires attention to what you eat and when you eat it (i.e., avoiding large meals in the evening).
- Drinking water helps to be hydrated properly.
- The quantity of caffeine intake affects the quality of sleep.
- You should reduce alcohol and avoid it one to two hours before hitting the pillow.
- Using phones and similar devices near sleep, affects our brain patterns, and that gets in the way of your brain moving into a recovery phase.
- Keeping a pen and paper beside you at night helps to let go if you wake with something on your mind.
- Regular exercise and therefore fitness, enables you to sleep better.
- You can catch up on sleep during the day, when managed in the right quantities and right time of the day.

However, bringing all that together is easier said than done. It is a chicken and egg thing. If you are not thinking properly or have little energy, you are less likely to make better choices. You are less likely to eat well, exercise, reduce alcohol, or stop binge scrolling video reels in the late hours. It is simply unrealistic. You need to get better quality sleep and give your brain the space to repair, before you are likely to make the changes that bring about better-quality sleep.

Quality sleep can still be absent even if you find ways to free your mind completely of all your concerns and commitments, as we'll explore in chapter twenty. You still need a means to switch off instantly to maximise the potential for recovery and repair. More repair enables better cognitive capacity during the day. That leads to better decisions. That leads to changes in behaviour and that leads to better quality sleep.

COACHING CORNER: Instant Sleep.

Mindfulness techniques are helpful in getting to sleep but are not for everyone. And, pushing thoughts away from your conscious mind still involves thinking. If you are not able to instantly switch off, try this technique for stopping thinking. After laying down and getting comfortable, close your eyes and look at the inside of your eye lids. Acknowledge the colours for a moment, then bring the focus of your eyes together. It is almost like crossing the eyes when making funny faces as a kid, but not to that point of it being painful. Repeating that slowly four or five times is generally enough. You'll know it is enough because you won't remember how many times you did it. Instead, you will fall asleep. This technique is especially useful if you are overtired, preoccupied, or want to take a twenty-minute power nap. With better quality sleep, comes better quality decisions, and that is where the truth to recovery rests.

Goals

Motivation to change, as further explored in chapter seventeen, is aided by alignment with more than one goal. Practicing a new behaviour or shedding a limiting belief is much easier when there are overlapping reasons. These crossed-over motivations reduce the chances of compromise when one aspect is achieved or not relevant anymore.

Furthermore, you need to be realistic about how you are motivated. Those who are externally motivated have an advantage. They can get others to keep them accountable to their goals. However, if you are intrinsically motivated you need to be realistic. That is because willpower isn't sufficient. While you may not need approval from others to know you are doing a good job, and perhaps you create measures or internal rewards, it is not enough. Thinking gets in the way. If you can rationalise yourself into doing something you can also talk yourself out of it. That overthinking can override the desire for change. Those who are intrinsically motivated need something else to bring about change in themselves. We will cover this further in Chapter twenty-one.

Winning

The process of bringing your body with you may have some unexpected benefits. The increase in fitness and energy will likely result in delivering a clearer mind, feeling less tired, making better eating and drinking choices, and perhaps improvements in other physical activities. Those better decisions compound. That has the potential to exponentially increase the benefit.

Bringing your body with you is a journey, not an end point. It isn't something that you do just today and not tomorrow. Attention to what you put in and what you do with your body is the key to physical wellbeing. With physical wellbeing you think clearer, and you engage more with every interaction and activity. All this gives you a better platform to achieve agency.

PART 4: MOMENTUM

Chapter 17: Hard work

Agency is more than just work.

Work

When you use the phrase 'work', what do you imply? What does using the word 'work' do to your attitude toward the things that have importance and meaning to you?

Do you associate the word 'work' with hard, demanding and unpleasant effort. What do people mean when they use the word 'hard' in relation to work that has no physical element? Would you consider it 'boring' in addition to being perceived as hard? Are there things that you must do day in and day out? Does the repetitive nature of that make it boring? Is it the absence of the novel, the new and exciting, part of the problem? Does it cause procrastination?

And what of sacrifice? Do you do things for the benefit of others? Is that always easy and enjoyable?

Also, what impression does it leave with those who look up to you? Perhaps a child might hear the word 'work', used repeatedly and negatively and then conclude, 'Mum tells me she must go to work. That takes her away from me. That makes me sad. Bad things make me sad, so work is a bad thing. I don't want to be sad when I grow up, so I won't do work like my mum.'.

Consider this question, 'Is everything you do new every time?'. The answer, is clearly no. Also, 'Do you do the same things ever?'. Of course you do. The reasons for the latter will include the need for some level of stability. It is also probable that some of the repetitive activities are not boring at all and even the complete opposite.

Consider of the things you must do that are difficult or hard, what happens when you overcome the challenge? Is there a sense of accomplishment, relief, and other positive emotions. Is there learning in there too?

So, therefore, is boredom just avoidance of what is hard, but worthwhile?

An alternative definition might be as per David Allen's writings. This definition of work is 'something that has meaning to you that isn't done yet'. In this definition 'work' may mean something necessary but not always enjoyable.

Change

In the field of psychology, motivation is a complex phenomenon that is driven by various internal and external factors. Competing drivers of motivation refer to situations where an individual faces multiple wants and needs. These pull them in different directions.

For instance, consider a student who has a passion for both art and science. On one hand, they are intrinsically motivated to pursue their artistic talents because it brings them joy and fulfilment. On the other hand, they may also be extrinsically motivated to excel in science due to the societal pressures and expectations of success in this field. These competing motivations can create a sense of conflict within the individual, making it challenging for them to decide which path to prioritize.

In such cases, the individual may experience a push-pull dynamic where they oscillate between the two competing motivations, trying to find a balance that satisfies both their internal desires and external expectations. This phenomenon is a common occurrence in many aspects of life, including career choices, personal relationships, and even daily decision-making processes.

The presence of competing motivation drivers can lead to increased stress and anxiety, as you struggle to reconcile your conflicting desires and make difficult choices. Understanding these drivers and the factors that influence them can be helpful in managing this stress and making more informed decisions that align with your values and goals.

For further details see *Immunity to Change: How to Overcome It and Unlock the Potential in Yourself and Your Organization*, by Robert Kegan and Lisa Laskow Lahey.

CIA

COACHING CORNER:CIA model

In the coaching world there is a model called 'CIA'. This model is presented by Neil Thompson and Sue Thompson in their 2008 book, *The Critically Reflective Practitioner*. The model is useful for breaking down complicated needs and wants. It has three elements, 'Control', 'Influence', and 'Accept'. The control element represents aspects of your situation that you can control (i.e., your thoughts, feelings, personal stuff, and physical actions). The influence element represents the aspects in your world that you can't control, but that you can bring some level of direction to, through your influence (i.e., where you have trust or authority). The accept element is for everything else (i.e., where you have no direct control or influence). The model is useful when you need to rationalize why you have resistance to a situation or choice. However, it misses the mark. you are never really in total control of everything. Nor are you truly able to guarantee the outcome through directing the actions of others. Life is just too complex.

Furthermore, even if you are doing something that is brave, failure to acknowledge the resistance puts you at risk. When you do not sense and acknowledge the resistance, you are in denial of it. An effective way to look at resistance is by looking at fear. While resistance is created from all our negative emotions, like disgust, boredom, hate, envy, sorrow, anger, frustration, discontentment, alarm, guilt, indifference, it is fear where we can see it clearly. To understand light, you must have dark. To understand agency, you must have resistance. To understand the resistance, you can explore the fear that holds you back: the fear of putting your views forward; the fear of asking for what you need; the fear of going after something you want; the fear of saying no, or the fear of letting go of something you have. Resistance isn't really about effort or work. There will always be things you don't feel like doing but must do, like cleaning the house, medical check-ups, or sharing sad news. At the core of the resistance is a conflict in your mind and heart as to the alignment of the experience to what you feel is right for yourself and for those you care about.

Breaking down your choices by 'Control', 'Influence', or 'Accept' sets you up for disappointment. This is because the 'accept' is always the fall back. Unfortunately, accepting something that isn't aligned to what you feel is right eventually grinds you down and that can turn to frustration and anger.

A better approach is to look at things slightly differently when you are trying to rationalize why you have resistance to a situation or choice. This still involves the use of the CIA acronym and the premise, but with different meaning given to the letters. 'C' is for 'Create my reality' and relates to actions you can take. These are the actions that will help you create the reality that you want, the person you want to be, and to create your physical, mental, and connected best self. Focus here brings direct benefit and experiences for yourself and those you care about. The 'I' is for 'Integrate my reality' and is one step back from actions that fit directly with your path. Integrating is about combining your and others' actions into a single shared reality (i.e., where there is a shared goal or direction, in partnership, team, or group situations). The final aspect is the 'A' and stands for 'Aligning my reality'. This is where you use the actions and experiences of others definition in bringing you closer to the reality you want and desire. It's about choosing to use the path set out by others to learn and grow. Examples would be joining a Camino Walk where someone else sets the path and pace, or playing a game with enthusiasm and vigour, using the odd rules defined by your child, or embracing the potential of an arranged marriage. Actions that integrate you with someone else's path and purpose, do help you. It is a form of Otherish Giving, as explored in chapter fifteen. This kind of giving brings benefit to others, without compromise to your own experience or wellbeing. In this way, engagement and alignment with your journey and ultimately your purpose, can be achieved in everything that you do and experience, no matter how much, or how little control or influence you have.

Chapter 18: The art of flying

Agency has direction.

Throw yourself at the ground and miss

The art of flying comes from *The Hitchhiker's Guide to the Galaxy*, which is a comedy science-fiction series created by Douglas Adams. It was initially developed for radio in the late 1970s, and then went into other formats including theatre, books, a TV series, video games, and films. The series centres around a book, The Hitchhiker's Guide to the Galaxy, which is a futuristic guidebook for intergalactic hitchhikers. The art of flying, or rather 'knack', as defined in The Hitchhiker's Guide to the Galaxy, is the ability to 'throw yourself at the ground and miss'. It is likely evident to you that you can't fly. The guide addresses this. The guide suggests that you can't fly because you are too deliberate in your focus. While plummeting through the air, it is likely that you won't be able to focus on anything else other than the fast-approaching hard ground. You won't let go of the idea of moving through the air and the potentially painful end. The trick, the guide suggests, is to be distracted at the crucial moment and then flying will just happen. The guide suggests that the mind, needs to feel this is all almost by accident. This is incredibly hard to do. The possibility of pain is just too great. Your mind will find it very difficult to let go of that. No matter how hard you try to focus elsewhere, at the back of your mind, in the dark recesses, there will be doubt linked to the fast-approaching ground. That doubtful thought might be miniscule in comparison to every other thought, but it is there. This has very powerful ramifications. If you want to truly 'fly', you need to track down the doubt and completely remove it. There is one further element to the art of flying. The guide suggests that if you find yourself accidentally hovering just above the ground, you risk having your experience further hampered by self-doubt. This is the idea that your self-doubt will tell you, 'Hey! You can't fly, you are not a bird!'. This message will be heard loud and clear, and your amygdala will lap it up. When that happens, you will continue to fail to miss the ground. We will look further at self-doubt later in the chapter.

Formula one racing car drivers are trained to focus away from where they are heading. Winning requires that they drive their cars fast, and at the limits. However, coming out of the straight with the car moving at its maximum speed, the last thing they want is a brick wall impeding their progress. Instead of focusing on the wall, they are trained to focus on the corner. They literally turn their heads and look at the corner. This is incredibly hard to do. The wall at the end of the straight is fast approaching and it is directly in their view. The car is shaking, the noise is tremendous, and everything is a blur. Yet, they still must turn their heads and look away from the impending very hard and unforgiving wall.

Taking the best path in life, and therefore reaching your potential, isn't always about focusing on what is straight in front of you. Like the art of flying or focusing on the corners, this is difficult. It's difficult because you have built your reality from what you already know and what is directly in front of you.

When you focus on the ground or on the concrete wall, that is what you get. These hard places represent your fears, your concerns, and your worries. Your fears might include not having enough things, money, friends, fitness, health, meaningful work, and love. When you focus on the absence (i.e., what you don't have), that is all you end up creating more of. You end up creating more of what you don't want and less of what you do. You simply get closer and closer to the hard and unforgiving places.

This is likely owing to a need to control things that get in the way of getting what you want. When you have invested time and effort, you need to feel that it wasn't all in vain. You need to know what you have built is sturdy and will remain in place. You trust in that level of certainty. This gives you comfort and the means to endure the crappy experiences confronting you daily. It's scary to consider that the idea that what you have built, must change before you can move forward. You cling to it and that holds you back. You cannot let go of the idea of 'the ground'. You have too much invested in it. Ground is important: your food comes from it; your workplaces use it; your home stands on it; your loved ones walk on it; and you need it to jump and to climb. You cannot simply detach yourself from your foundations. And you simply can't ignore them while plummeting toward them.

Focus forms the path

Focus creates your reality. It puts you into the experiences that form every moment of your life. Neuroscience, the scientific study of our nervous system, tells us that our thinking is aided by a complicated set of pathways in our brain. These pathways link the sensors and the memories we have of our worlds. We use these pathways to react and behave. Some pathways are so well used that we need very little thought to engage them. They basically trigger automatically. Like driving the car home from work and getting to the driveway and being unable to remember large parts of the trip. More on neuroscience can be found in the works of Amy Brann (See Brann, Amy; *Neuroscience for Coaches* (2015)). Brann shows that we now have evidence of how we can understand and change our behaviours and beliefs.

It is entirely possible to create new pathways in your mind so that events trigger completely different behaviours. You can replace behaviours that are not in your best interest. You could retrain your default behaviour to do something different. An example being how you react to a mean comment from someone you must interact with on a regular basis. You could retrain yourself to handle the remark with ease and calm, instead of fighting back. Just like a dirt track across a field, if you don't think too hard, you will simply follow the track, even if it takes you away from where you want to be. Unlike tracks in a field, which can be washed away over time, the tracks in our minds are very difficult to remove. However, we can create new ones. You can put yourself at the gate (i.e., the trigger point), and forge a new path across the field. While it takes time for the new track to become your default preference, it can be done. You simply need to make it more prominent and easier to 'fall into' than the old track. Once achieved, the new track will be your normal path across the field. The old track will still be there; however, it won't be as easy to find. Retraining our brains to behave differently, operates the exact same way. When you purposefully behave differently long enough, it will become automatic. That focused effort pays dividends. It enables agency.

Choosing to fly

Your state of mind attracts experiences that either bring you toward or further away from what you want.

Your experiences take you further away from what brings meaning when you find yourself in a place of high resistance. This is a place where you feel unable to influence your choices: a place where you feel others are in your way and are to blame for something that doesn't feel right; a place where you blame others and other things for the undesired outcomes of your choices; a place where your self-talk suggests you are powerless (i.e., 'I am alone', 'I have no money', 'my sex life is non-existent', 'I have no energy', 'I have a crap job', or 'My children never do what I ask').

Your experiences take you toward what brings meaning, when you believe in yourself and your ability to choose. This is a place where you proactively engage in your choices. It is a place where you positively accept the outcomes of your choices, and the learning opportunities contained within. It is a place where you truly believe in free will (i.e., 'I am loved', 'I have had some wonderful experiences', 'I am playful', 'I am determined', 'I am a thoughtful co-worker', or 'I am a caring parent').

The consequences of this are significant. Existing in a place where you have high resistance brings only further experiences that create more resistance. It's a downward spiral. However, existing in a place of belief in your own choices, brings more choice. It brings more opportunities to experience and learn. It brings more of everything.

Unstuck

Experiencing yourself or someone else losing it, is not pleasant. Acting erratically, or oddly, is a sign that you have lost your way, even if just temporarily. Stress and pressure often get the blame, but there is another factor. When you have been self-absorbed and doubting your own capabilities, you can come unstuck. When you believe in yourself and what you can give to others, you build momentum. In other words, when the amygdala is not being managed effectively, you can find yourself at the mercy of your freeze, flight, or fight response.

When you are in control of your thinking and managing the amygdala effectively, you bring intention to your aim, and that gets you to where you want to be. A simple example of this can be found in moving around other people (i.e., getting into a lift or going through doors). What happens when you are drifting aimlessly in self-pity, doubt, or worry? Do you find that you do not take their needs into consideration when you meet at the door at the same time. Do you find yourself oblivious to others until you awkwardly bump into them.

It is exhausting dwelling in a place of anger, frustration, and envy. This place is detrimental to your ability to function and be productive. And yet, it is a comforting place. Perhaps it is somewhere that things in your mind make sense. Equally, distancing yourself from the challenges that you face, through blame, can make things easier to cope with. Perhaps you have had good reason. Perhaps you've struggled financially. Or experienced knock back after knock back. Perhaps you struggled in your relationships. Perhaps there had been illness and loss. Maybe there have been times when you have found yourself totally miserable and struggling to figure out what went wrong. No matter what hardships you have endured, dwelling in that negative place can be draining and a downward spiral. Picking yourself up after these types of experiences isn't something to be taken lightly. However, while not easy at times, it is achievable if you are intentional with your aim.

While it may be obvious that things get harder when you avoid focusing on what you are doing and where you are, maintaining that focus isn't easy. At times, it is easier to avoid taking aim. Perhaps you let fear of that thing not happening, hold you back. Perhaps you can't let go of the idea of failing. For example, looking at an empty bank account and holding the fear that a better job may never happen, simply leaves you where you are, looking at an empty bank account. When in that fearful place, you don't focus on driving actions that get you closer to landing a better job. Instead, perhaps you take a step back and coast, miss opportunities, get let go or even fired.

It is said that we can have whatever we focus on. This concept does not always sit well at times because so much of what we aim at, does not materialize. The reason for this is unexpected, but obvious. The reason is that we confuse the thing that actually happened, with what we thought we wanted.

Many of the things that happen to us happen because we wanted it, either intentionally, or not. For example, perhaps you would like to live in a huge house with loads of rooms and vast lawns and gardens. However, perhaps you also think that you don't want to spend every waking moment cleaning and gardening. Nor do you want to spend every moment working, away from loved ones, making the big bucks so you can afford to have someone else do the cleaning and gardening for you. What you actually want is something quite different than a big house with sprawling gardens. Let's explore some other examples. If you want to have a fit and adventurous girlfriend/boyfriend/spouse, are you prepared to be fit and adventurous as well? Also, are you willing to manage the attention that you get from others? If you want a life full of travel and new experiences, are you willing to sacrifice the time with the friends and family you leave behind? If you want your kids raised in the idyllic countryside with lots of space and nature, and to enjoy it with them, are you willing to sacrifice your income and career development opportunities? If you want to have a fit firm body capable of running marathons, are you willing to sacrifice the time with loved ones so you can go to the gym all the time and run the miles needed to get there and stay there? If you want to be engaged in all manner of community giving projects, are you willing to sacrifice the time with your spouse and children?

You may think what you are doing is moving you in the direction you want. However, if your focus is on actions oriented towards avoidance, that is what you will get. You will get something that is not the life you think you want. You will get something that falls far short of it.

Giving the Attention Muscle attention

An essential aspect of your ability to focus is what can be metaphorically called your 'attention muscle'. This concept simplifies the complex functions of brain areas like the Prefrontal Cortex, Parietal Cortex, Thalamic Reticular Nucleus, and Inferior Frontal Junction, which are involved in managing attention.

The 'attention muscle' metaphor helps us understand how to observe our emotions and thoughts more effectively. It is like having an 'inner voice' that guides you in using your cognitive resources wisely. A well-developed attention muscle enables you to remain calm and connected even in the face of adversity. This means you can:

- Regulate your emotions and thoughts.
- Engage appropriately with complex situations without reacting impulsively, such as lashing out or withdrawing when faced with challenges or opposition.

In essence, strengthening your 'attention muscle' helps you respond to life's trials with thoughtful action rather than knee-jerk reactions.

COACHING CORNER: Strengthening the attention muscle.

It is unlikely that anyone is born with a fully developed attention muscle. For most, the lacking in this capability will be evident from simply looking at erratic behaviours, more so in childhood and adolescence, but also at times in adulthood. Few naturally have strong capabilities in the realms of emotional and thinking control. Most must learn and develop it.

One way to strengthen your attention muscle, as mentioned in chapter fourteen, is simply the art of catching the emotion by naming it in your head, quietly to yourself. Once you name the emotion, you have engaged the thinking part of your brain and put the amygdala back to sleep. You may still choose to lash out or withdraw, but you will do it consciously and in the right measure.

Another technique is the idea of clearing the brain of thought. This technique is part of what many experience when practicing mindfulness. Clearing the mind of thought is hard to achieve and requires lots of practice. The idea of clearing the mind of thought is simply the idea of thinking of nothing. This is not the 'thinking of nothing' that surfaces when a significant other asks you 'what are you thinking?' and you reply with 'nothing' simply because you don't want to share your thoughts. Or the 'thinking of nothing' that happens when you are letting your mind wander around from one thought to the next. No, mindfulness related 'thinking of nothing' is when you consciously put the mind in a totally open space ready for the next thought or input. Typically, this isn't a place that remains open and free for very long, but it'll be just long enough for you to observe the moment of nothing. The process of observing and then clearing the thought is the activity that strengthens the attention muscle.

Clearing the mind of thought is encapsulated in David Allen's work relating to *Capturing What has Your Attention*. This is the idea of externalizing absolutely everything that has your attention. It is a crucial step in David Allen's approach to achieving stress-free productivity, which is better known as 'Getting Things Done' (GTD). The practice of clearing the mind of everything of importance and putting it into external places where you will be reminded of at the appropriate time, also strengthens your attention muscle.

The technique of noticing what has your attention can be done in all kinds of situations. You can do it when on your own, when with others or even when engaged in physical activity, like running. You simply notice when your mind wanders onto some thought unrelated to what is happening around you. When that happens, you give it a slight nudge to see if it will drift away. Most thoughts will. If it doesn't, you can use a simple test to determine what you will do next. The test involves asking yourself, 'Have I had this thought before?'. If you have had it before and you don't want to continue enjoying it, you externalize it. This means you put the thought somewhere for you to process later. Perhaps you write it down or record it into a note taking app on your phone. Once the idea is externalized, you should be able to return to giving your full attention to whatever you were doing prior to the distracting thought.

A very simple way to build the attention muscle is to take a couple of minutes each day, to practice observing your attention. You can do this by focusing on an object, like a ballpoint pen or pencil. While doing that, you push out any thoughts that drift in and return to focusing on the object.

Both naming emotions and thinking of nothing techniques, get easier the more they are practiced. Eventually clearing the mind or naming emotions will happen automatically. It is through practice that you will be better able to manage where you focus your attention.

Aim—'ask and listen'

As explored in chapter seventeen, competing drivers of motivation may cause you to find yourself on a path that doesn't appear to be where you want to be. At times you will get pulled or pushed slightly off track. The experiences and situations that result feel like they weren't what you thought you wanted. When that happens, you can choose to use these misaligned experiences to learn more about yourself.

When something doesn't quite go to plan, you can stop for a moment and be curious. You can take in where you are. You can ask yourself, what it is about this moment that is important to you. You can listen for the thoughts that come with that question. The experience that you really want might be near, perhaps to the left or right or just behind you.

When you cling to what isn't what you want, you get blocked and stuck. You compromise your ability to think clearly. However, when you let go using the ask and listen approach, you see what is about you. You see the sun peeking through the clouds, so to speak. You become curious to the potential of where you are.

With a strong attention muscle, it is easier to focus, and that drives your actions. Taking aim in a meaningful manner is far easier when you manage your focus and attention. It is far easier to slow down and listen, rather than think deeply about what is missing or what went wrong. Often actions are made because of fear. Perhaps you put actions and plans in place to avoid something bad happening. While taking a spear into the jungle is important, actions made based on what is missing can keep you from your path. When you are in control of your focus, you can listen. You hear what actions are important and aligned with what you want, even if you don't quite know what that is yet. From there, the actions you take bring you closer to actual aim.

COACHING CORNER: Asking and listening.

The process of asking and listening, can be summarised as follows:

1. At any moment, be it when things are going well or when they are not, ask yourself, 'What actions will bring me closer to what I want and need?'.
2. After asking, pay attention to the thoughts that show up. Use the responses you get from listening, to drive your actions.

During this process be sure to give yourself some room to explore and to be wrong. You can't be expected to have all the answers and get everything right. Forgiveness is the key to learning. If you keep control of your thinking, you'll get plenty of signposts along the way. From there you can correct your path. You may not find yourself literally soaring through the air, but it will feel close to it.

Chapter 19: The riptide is both friend and foe

Agency is a wild ride.

Surfing

Surfing, when done well, is an exhilarating experience. When not, it is exhausting and underwhelming. There isn't anything pleasant about getting caught in the white water, colliding with other surfers, reefs or rocks, and having entanglements with less than friendly marine life. On top of all of that, there is the added challenge of paddling against powerful swell. If you want to maximise your experience, you need to get in the vicinity of good waves. Here lies the challenge. To get onto good and powerful waves, you need to get into them. Jet skis can help in that regard, but for most, it is the strength of your arms that matter. This is where the riptide comes into play. Those who have spent time at a beach will have inevitably come across warnings about the dangers of these fast-moving water flows. For surfers, the riptide is a blessing, not a curse.

The riptide is basically the beach's method of releasing the energy in the waves. There is immense energy within waves as they reach the shallow waters of the beach. This needs to be released. The riptides are sections of water where that energy bounces back out to sea. Every surf beach has them. The nature and force of these riptides is vastly dependent on the shape of the beach, water depth, and the power of the waves. In some places that surge of water going back out to sea is gentle and of low impact. In other places, the flow of water is fast and dramatic.

For the unaware swimmer, getting caught in that fast and dramatic flow of the riptide can be catastrophic. In no time at all a novice swimmer can be a good distance out to sea in cold water and beyond their swimming capacity to return to shore. However, for the experienced surfer, the riptide is an essential element in performing well. Firstly, a strong riptide equates to powerful waves. Strong waves are key to an engaging experience. Secondly, paddling back into big powerful waves is exhausting and just not realistic. So, experienced surfers use the riptides to get back out to sea. They then catch waves back to shore. These surfers know how to get out of the riptides at the right time. This knowledge allows them to put themselves into the optimal place to catch the next great wave.

In summary, the riptide is both friend and foe. For some, the riptide is a threat to their very existence. For others, it is pivotal in how they realise their potential.

Less resistance

The riptide friend or foe metaphor represents the skills and experience you utilise. When you master the riptide, or the skills you need, life becomes engaging and has less resistance in it. When you try to do things without the needed skills, you face hardship, pain, and even death. However, you don't arrive on the planet knowing how to have exhilarating experiences in surf. You learn it.

When the stakes are high, we want to take caution. Rushing into the surf and the riptides to experience surfing, isn't a great idea if you can't swim. It puts outcome above everything. This strategy misses the opportunity for learning. Not going into the water at all is pretty much the same thing. It too misses the opportunity for learning. Looking at challenges in terms of doing it without caution or not at all, is an absolute. It is an optimistic verses pessimistic mindset trade-off. The trade-off leaves no room for error and learning. A better strategy is to approach things gradually. This involves testing the water, learning about its characteristics, and seeing how you might engage. You build skills gradually, without drowning. You put yourself in the path of resistance at the right measures.

The white water

In reality, learning to surf is about spending lots of time battling the white water, the foaming mess after a wave breaks. It can be frustrating and not that much fun, especially if you keep getting dumped. However, losing sight of the role it plays in the learning process inhibits you from mastering surfing.

It is true that taking aim is crucial. You need to have direction. You need to have goals to strive for. However, it is not just about setting aims. Even when your aims are clear, you aren't always right. As explored in chapter ten, you simply can't predict the future. Sticking hard and fast to a plan is limiting. You need to be flexible. As explored in chapter eleven, you need to learn from your mistakes. Equally, you need to flex and adjust when things are seemingly ok. Failing is just one indicator that you are off course. You will also see signposts when you are having fun and engaging experiences. Those too can be taking you off course.

Learning is a gradual process. It requires engagement and it requires reflection. Momentum is the key. Small steps, one after another, are best. And during the experience, be it failing, or succeeding, you must look and observe. You need to look for the learning opportunity.

Shedding the shell

The process of major transformation is challenging and can expose you to distraction and dilution. Timely, appropriate and quality outcomes are more likely when you fully engage in a process of re-alignment that involves safeguards to protect vulnerabilities.

The idea of re-alignment is not unlike the process a rock lobster goes through as it grows. For a rock lobster to grow, it must shed its shell and grow a new one. This process is painful and risky. It is painful in that the old shell becomes increasingly uncomfortable as the lobster out grows it. Before shedding the old shell, the lobster first finds a rock to hide under. Once the old shell is gone, the real challenge begins. This is because while growing its new shell it is vulnerable. The rock is crucial for protection if the lobster has any chance of getting the new shell grown before it gets discovered.

As with the rock lobster, the same is true of your own development. To grow you must shed and then replace the beliefs and behaviours which served you well, but which are no longer as relevant in the new context.

The process of shedding and replacing beliefs and behaviours is not straightforward. It is a challenge to face down your old beliefs and behaviours, especially the ones that protect you from harm. You may also suffer from the idea that they got you thus far so they will continue to aid your progress. History has proven that this is often not the case. So, while there may be a huge sense of relief and celebration when you overcome desires to hold onto limiting beliefs, for a period afterwards you are vulnerable. As well as a potential sense of loss or awkwardness, you also become vulnerable to distraction and dilution as you strive to adopt your new behaviours.

As with the lobster, you also need your own version of the 'rock' to protect you as you breakdown and reframe the beliefs that have shaped you. You need support to help you build new beliefs that are better suited to the complexity and context that you find yourself in. At a more fundamental level, you also need support when you get stuck or challenged. You need the support to keep you motivated to get to a better place and build that new and stronger self. This process is achievable on your own, through reading, training, and trial and error. The process, however, is greatly aided by engaging with others to help (i.e., coaches, counsellors, therapists, and the right type of friends).

A note of caution with respect to getting help from non-professionals, especially, loved ones. Unfortunately, some of those close to you might be linked to the old shell. Inviting them 'under the rock' too soon can be detrimental and potentially fatal. This is typically the case if those loved ones haven't shed their old shells. They might not fully appreciate the new place you are moving into. They may use your vulnerability to their advantage. Some people aren't ready to face their own demons and will push back if you try to shed yours in their presence. The Social Needs Relationship Matrix, as explored in chapter fifteen, can be very helpful in this process.

Riding the wave

A lot of what will come to you when you ask and then listen, as explored in chapter eighteen, will relate to shifting behaviours that you hold dear. A useful tip in this process is to search for the learning that serves you and others.

COACHING CORNER: Searching for limiting behaviours.

When searching for behaviours that need changing, ask yourself:
- Does this serve me?
- Does this serve others?
- Does this feel right?

Ask those questions when you are unsure about a choice you are making. Ask them of your routines and habits as well as the commitments you have made to yourself, to others, and your communities. Ask these questions when you are in the middle of an engaging experience. Take care to check that what comes back isn't based on high resistance, like fear, or avoidance. Do this by asking yourself if what you are thinking about, involves changing someone else's behaviour or projecting one of your own beliefs on them. As we will explore more in chapter twenty-one, ego is therefore the driver. When you get an answer like this, ask again. And, once more, listen. With time, this process will bring you to a conclusion that feels right and good. Focus your time and energy there.

When really stuck, ask yourself, 'What could I do now that would serve me and others?'. Then listen again and apply the same process of checking for high resistance.

Riding the big waves of life is fun, but not without risk. And big waves are scary. You may get hurt or even go under. Waves in life put you under pressure, but the engagement is electric and the potential for growth is unmatched. You must not be afraid to get into the water, take the riptide, and look for waves to ride! However, you also must be focused in your preparation and in the engagement during the experience. This happens when you pay attention, and when you ask and listen. The key is to stay with your own truth and not to take things at face value. You must engage in the waves of life because you never really know what will happen next.

Focusing on the experience, not the outcome is where the truth can be found. Riding that awesome wave is great, but the meaning is actually in the paddling out, the searching, the choice to get in the right place for the wave, the anticipation, the fear, the push to get into the wave as it forms, then the launch onto your feet and the rush that comes with it. And it is in the afters; the feelings of what was achieved and the sharing of the experience with others.

Chapter 20: Mastery

Agency thrives in reality.

Right thing, Right way, Right time

The art of agency is the process of covering more ground with minimal additional effort. It is about staying in touch with the now, at the same time as getting yourself further along the path in an efficient manner.

The opposite of the art of agency is getting caught up in whatever you are doing without due care about where it is taking you and what havoc you are leaving in your wake. Examples of this would include taking on too much and then letting others down. Another example would be generating effort for your future self because you did something badly just to get it across the line. A final example would be the allowance others have to make around you, so that you can 'do your thing' (i.e., others compromising things for themselves for your success or picking up after you).

The art of agency is not easy. It takes focus and it isn't a 'one size fits all' kind of thing. You need to find an approach that works for you. A good place to start that explorative journey is with focus on doing the right things, the right way, and at the right time. David Allen's GTD framework is a good place to start in that regard. On top of the learning there, you need an appreciation of beliefs and behaviours, and the underlying values and traits. The latter helping you take the right perspective, at the right time.

What follows, in this chapter, is one approach to help make sense of it all and engage fully with everything that has importance. The content here is proposed as one possible solution to freeing the psyche of our daily burdens. Below you will find coverage of the five aspects of the art of agency: presence, awareness, crafting, accountability and focus.

Mastery in presence

Mastery in presence is essential if you are to stay on top of your emotions and keep your thinking brain in the driver's seat. Presence is also an essential ingredient in realizing meaning.

Presence, in the context of your mind, simply means being aware of what has your attention. Eckhart Tolle suggests that presence is the intentional focus on engagement in the present moment through awareness of thought not thought itself.

Having skills in presence serves three purposes:

- Firstly, it aids in your ability to observe your emotions and respond appropriately to them.
- Secondly, it helps you direct your thinking capacity.
- Thirdly, it assists with short-term management of chronic stress, excessive worry, overthinking, preoccupation and other related derailing conditions.

When you are not aware of what has your attention, you risk getting drawn into the things that are in front of you (i.e., the latest or loudest things). This is not unlike waving a shiny toy in front of a baby to distract them from whatever is causing them grief. While those things may be still important, they might not be the most important thing for you to be focused on at that moment. Furthermore, the latest and loudest things in front of you, will generally have greater importance for others than you. While this is a rewarding pursuit, focusing on what is important for others, can leave you neglecting yourself. It is said that, if you do not manage how you use your time and energy, someone else will manage it for you.

In practical terms, presence is about not having the same thought twice, unless it is a thought you want to continue enjoying. Instead, as explored in Chapter seventeen, you must externalise repeating thoughts to a trusted place. We will explore externalising below in mastery in crafting. This concept is presented within the works of David Allen and the idea of GTD step one, Capture.

Here are some examples of the absence of presence:

1. Holding in your head, the things you need to do ahead of the next monthly meeting.
2. Continually reminding yourself of that gift that needs getting by the weekend.
3. Going over repeatedly the sequence of steps needed to complete a report.
4. Repeating again and again out loud the places the kids need to be delivered to this weekend.

Continually thinking about these things (i.e., reminding yourself constantly because they are too important to forget), not only uses the limited supply of brain fuel, but it also reduces your ability to keep crazy at bay. David Rock, in his book *Your Brain at Work*, as we looked at in chapter thirteen, explains this final piece well. He labels this challenge as *The Stage Needs a Lot of Lighting*. To see the actors clearly, you need strong and bright lights. That requires a lot of energy and unfortunately that energy is very limited. Quality sleep is the main place you get this fuel for your brain. Furthermore, it is evident that you have a maximum of four hours of brain fuel after a good night's sleep. Using this limited supply of energy on reminders and rethinking is unnecessary and wasteful. It leaves you mentally exhausted and largely numb until you sleep again and recharge.

It is important to clarify that being present and fully engaged, is not the same as being 'disconnected' or 'offline'. It is just not realistic to suggest you can disconnect or go-offline and still be productively engaged in the modern world. You need connectivity, social media, and engagement in order to get things done. While possible, most will struggle to be productively engaged by having long 'connected' verses 'disconnected' periods (i.e., connected on Monday through Friday, 9am to 5pm, and disconnected at all other times). The key is to manage your thinking limitations and not fight them. This is the idea of being 'switched on'. It is the idea of being appropriately engaged with everything that has meaning to you at all times. This means you are fully present. This does require some rigor and discipline when it comes to certain technology and social media.

At the heart of presence is the attention muscle, as explored in chapter eighteen. The benefits of strengthening the attention muscle, go far beyond emotional intelligence and just keeping crazy at bay. Having the ability to manage your thinking is a crucial element in doing stuff. As David Rock suggests that your conscious capacity is miniscule in comparison to your unconscious capacity. He suggests that while it seems unlikely that you can control when you have an insight, strengthening the attention muscle can dramatically increase the likelihood that an insight will emerge.

Mastery in awareness

Mastery in awareness is necessary to focus your attention on the most important thing. It also aids you in processing your emotions and making decisions about them. The latter being an essential ingredient in keeping your attention where you want it.

Mastery in awareness gives you the ability to isolate the level of importance.

Having skills in awareness serves two purposes:

- Firstly, it aids in your ability to know how to best use your limited time and energy.
- Secondly, it aids in your ability to respond appropriately to your emotions.

You make decisions all the time. To make decisions you draw on your beliefs, you consider context, and you use your experiences. To speed things up, you form habits around decisions you make frequently so you don't need to rethink them each time. These habits give you some space to tackle the less frequently occurring new things that require you to consider and make choices about. These new things are in what you see, smell, feel, touch, and hear. Furthermore, the things you already know, bounce around your head, and create opportunities for more choices. The quality of the life you create (i.e., where you put yourself and what you do when you are there), is directly related to your ability to make good choices. Awareness is the construct or premise on which you make your choices. Mastery in awareness enables you to make the choices that have you doing more of the right things, in the right way, and at the right time.

Mastery in awareness is addressed in part within David Allen's idea of GTD step two, Clarify. However, there is more to it than just following a workflow. Step two, Clarify crosses over into mastery in crafting as explored below. In terms of mastery in awareness, while workflow is important, knowing your values and traits, and therefore knowing the basis on which you really make decisions, is crucial.

A further deepening of understanding comes when you considered GTD step two, Clarify, in the context of Essentialism, a concept that is wonderfully articulated by Greg McKeown in his 2014 book, *Essentialism. The Disciplined Pursuit of Less*. McKeown's idea of Essentialism is all about figuring out what is truly important in your life or work, and then cutting out all the stuff that isn't. It's like cleaning your room: you keep only the things that you really need or love and get rid of all the clutter. By doing this, you make more room for what truly matters, and your life or work becomes simpler and better focused. Essentialism promotes the need to better understand how you are making decisions about where you put yourself and what you do when you get there. McKeown also looks at what causes successful people to fail. In summary, he suggests that success brings more options and opportunities, which can lead to spreading yourself too thin. That diffusion results in failure.

Mastery in awareness can be tested as follows: when a request arrives or when you have a thought, can you answer it immediately with a yes or no? That is, you don't procrastinate or deliberate over the answer. Rather, it is immediately clear to you if you will or won't engage with the request. The choice may be qualified, but it will be clear. For example, you might answer with 'yes' and qualify it with, 'but not until next month'. Equally, you might answer with a 'No' and qualify it with, 'I need more information about BLANK before I will do this.'. When delivering a 'no' to others requesting something of you, you might use a Graceful No as outlined by McKeown. We'll get to more of that shortly. All these are still clear and immediate decisions. The speed at which you can answer with a clear decision, is the test. This is because, if you have been diligently building mastery in awareness, you are already in touch with your priorities and goals, and also appropriately engaged with everything else that already has importance to you.

To realise mastery, you need to have a great relationship with 'Yes' and 'No'. This idea speaks largely to the decision and processing workflow proposed in GTD step two, Clarify. The workflow starts with the question of 'What is it?'. This question primes your mind around the level of importance. The next question is 'Is it Actionable?'. There are only two choices at this point, 'yes' or 'no'. The 'yes' choice implies that you will take responsibility for moving this forward immediately. The 'no' choice means that you will not. The 'no' choice is also acceptance that for now, there is no need to spend further precious mental thinking capacity and qualify it further.

Allen's take on 'Yes' and 'No' is just the beginning.

Firstly, perspective has an impact and that gives you room to say no, as per McKeown's Graceful No. This is where you leave a request elsewhere, with the requester, or with the community where that thing originated. An example being, where you pause for longer than you would normally in the hope the requester will take the hint and withdraw the request. Another example would be where you say 'Yes, if you do xyz first.' Another example would be if you say, 'I can't help, but so-and-so might if you ask them.'. And one final example is, if you were to say, 'I cannot right now, but I might be able to when I finish xyz.' The Graceful No is a 'no' from your perspective but a 'yes' from the perspective of the person asking. Leaving it somewhere else or leaving it to someone else to progress, doesn't mean you can't be involved, but you are putting the ownership for taking responsibility somewhere else.

Secondly, time has an impact on 'yes' and 'no'. That is, you might decide something has importance to you, but you are not going to move it forward until next summer. This is in a way a 'Yes', but also a 'No'. Ultimately, this choice is down to the level of importance and the context of your current situation.

To get better at understanding the level of importance, you need to know your values and traits (i.e., the core of your personality as looked at in chapter thirteen).

Furthermore, from your understanding of your values, you build methods to efficiently determine the level of importance. McKeown suggests you need to establish minimum and maximum criteria for choosing where you focus your attention. The minimum criteria demark what causes you always to say no. The maximum criteria are your stretch goals. From there you aim to hit some of these in any choice. In summary, in choosing yes, you must satisfy all the minimum and some of the maximum criteria.

Mastery in awareness is very much like mastery in presence, in that it's not a tangible skill. Mastery in awareness doesn't show up like striking the ball to get that winning goal or finding the words that close the sale. Mastery is only evident over time; in that you see it by looking back on what you did and feeling it in the moments when you put yourself in the right place. Unfortunately, and just like mastery in presence, if you do not master awareness your ability to craft, exercise accountability, and be focused, will be vastly compromised and, in some cases, completely in vain.

Mastery in crafting

Mastery in crafting is important if you want to perform at your best. You use this skill to make efficient use of your thinking capacity.

Crafting is important because if not applied, you risk underutilizing your two most precious resources—time and energy. Neglecting to use your available time and energy in the most meaningful manner makes it much harder to live up to your expectations and choose the path that you want.

David Allen describes the idea behind crafting when he explores GTD step three, Organize. Allen looks at the idea that outcomes of your decisions must be externalized (i.e., recorded or written down). And that you must externalize to places that you trust so that the things that have meaning for you are available to you when you need them. This is the idea that the things that have meaning are where they need to be when they need to be there. In other words, you are 'being organized' when you have not made life harder for your future self.

Chris Bailey, in his 2016 book *The Productivity Project: Proven Ways to Become more Awesome*, does a great job of articulating the risk of borrowing from your future self. This is the idea that when you procrastinate, you are creating work for yourself in the future, or worst still, someone else. For example, when you come in from an adventure and dump the equipment in a pile, you are creating work for yourself when you need it next. Another example would be dropping or saving a report haphazardly somewhere and then having to spend time later trying to find it again. As Allen puts it, the idea here is to consider things 'when they show up, not when they blow up'. We aren't talking about doing everything as it shows up. No, crafting in this context is simply that, for things that have meaning, you do whatever is required now to ensure that you can do what is required later.

Here are some more examples of where mastery in crafting applies:

- You create the space where you can work deeply (i.e., you switch off devices, disable popup notifications, resist the temptation to check for email and social media updates).
- You create the means to save the outcomes of your thinking, both physical, and electronic, i.e., you have trusted places to externalise your thinking.
- You organize the outcomes of your decisions (i.e., the results of isolating the level of importance).
- You capture thoughts as they occur to you, and not let them fester in your mind, i.e., you externalise repeating thoughts, as well as your worries, overthinking and preoccupations.
- You put things where they belong, so you can find them easily, later.

COACHING CORNER: Mastery in crafting.

To achieve mastery in crafting, you need to be doing the following:

Aspect 1: Maintain a list of aims (i.e., use a Projects list).

An aim, in this context, is something that you are committed to moving towards, in the present moment. David Allen uses the term 'project'. Allen suggests that a project is something that has more than one step, where the steps are not self-evident from the outcome and where that outcome is expected to be realized in a year or less. Self-evident means that you understand the steps needed to realize the outcome. Some self-evident examples might be: (1) fill the stapler (assuming you have a well-stocked stationery cupboard); (2) mow the lawn (assuming you have a working mower, and it isn't raining); and (3) Collect Mum & Dad from the airport. The steps here should be self-evident, so there is no need to maintain a separate project listing. In Allen's approach, anything longer than a year is really a goal or a focus area.

Aspect 2: Maintain lists of decisions that you have made about what you will do (i.e., use a list of next actions)

A next action is something that you can do now, or anytime from now, and that will move a project closer to achieving the desired outcome. Many confuse the concept of 'Tasks' with next actions. They are not the same. For example, you can't 'do' a 'Weekly Report', that is a task. You can, however, open last week's report and prepare it for making changes. This is a specific action that you can do now.

Aspect 3: Maintain accurate records of all date and time commitments, (i.e., use a calendar diary).

It sounds obvious, but it surprising how often people rely on their memories for date and time commitments, especially for personal commitments. As things get complex, with a spouse, and children, it is just unrealistic that you will remember every date and time you have committed to doing something for yourself or others.

Aspect 4: Maintain a later start list.

A later start list is a list of things that you can't start now, or things for which it doesn't make sense to start now. For example, 'renew passport' is not something that makes sense to start just after you have got a new passport. But it will be something important to do as the current passport approaches its expiry date.

Aspect 5: Maintain a list of things that you are not going to do right now (i.e., use a someday/maybe list).

If you are mastering awareness, it will be easy to know what you will do now and what you won't. However, you will struggle to let go of it unless you are sure that you will get back to it at some point. David Allen refers to this as a 'Someday Maybe List'. Another way to think of it is the idea of 'Deferred Decisions'. Either way, this list is for those things that are important in that they have meaning for you, but not just right now given the other things you know about that need your attention.

Aspect 6: At all times, externalise your repeating thoughts, as well as your worries, overthinking and preoccupations.

Holding onto thoughts of what you need, want or should do reduces your thinking capacity and your ability to focus. In practice, externalising involves physical and electronic 'inboxes' to capture your thoughts in the moment. As outlined in aspect seven, below, these inboxes must be cleared to zero (i.e., processed) at the appropriate intervals, and the results of those decisions inserted into your lists as outlined in other aspects of mastery in crafting.

Furthermore, allowing worries, overthinking and preoccupations, excessive access to your thinking space, isn't productive and does nothing to help you move forward. As eluted to in chapter twelve, while chronic stress, excessive worry, overthinking, preoccupation and other related derailing conditions aren't things to be taken lightly, you have a choice in the short-term. You can choose to manage the moment and engage with what is in your immediate control. This is achieved by using a journal to write down the worries. Journalling makes it easier for you to step back from them, acknowledge where you are and hopefully find what will help you move forward, in the short-term. The journal can be electronic, like a note taking app in your phone or an integrated environment like Microsoft OneNote. Paper works just as well. When choosing the paper journal, be sure to choose a basic journal. Avoid fancy journals that might have you thinking you need to write eloquently. No, for this aspect of externalising your worries, a simple journal is best where you feel you can write anything and in any manner. The final chapter includes some questions that might help when reviewing your written thoughts.

Aspect 7: At predefined intervals, look in all the places you have collected stuff and make decisions about the level of importance.

At regular intervals, perhaps daily, you must review the things you have captured. These items need to be processed. You need to apply mastery in awareness to make choices about the level of importance and then organise the outcomes appropriately. The items to be processed will include physical things, emails, social media updates, news, other forms of instant messaging and of course, thoughts. Also known as unfinished thinking, these new things may be important to you. You need to ensure you spend time deciding what these things mean. You need to consider if you are going to do something with them. Regular and frequent attention to processing is important because if the stacks of new things or unfinished thinking, gets too big, you won't go near them anymore.

Unfortunately, when it comes to mastery in crafting, the devil is in the detail. Sometimes you must roll up your sleeves and get it done. Achieving mastery in the skill of crafting is largely about forming habits. You won't do it just with a desire to be more disciplined. Instead, you must trick yourself with reminders and external accountability to keep up the required rigor until habits form.

Mastery in accountability

Mastery in accountability ensures you are appropriately engaged with the decisions you have made about what is important. In other words, you reflect on and review the thinking you have already done so you don't forget to follow through on commitments to yourself and others.

While the whole idea of the art of agency can't be realized without mastery in all five skills, the skill of accountability is crucial and is the aspect that is often the hardest to apply and master.

Having a healthy mind and body and delivering meaning (i.e., being the best that you can be), takes time and effort. You need to apply yourself to make the changes that will drive you forward and keep up the momentum. Crucial to that, is being accountable to yourself for the decisions you have already made. You run the risk of all your efforts being in vain if you don't take that accountability seriously. You stand to waste all your effort on capturing what has your attention, making decisions about what is important and organizing those decisions.

David Allen describes the idea behind accountability when he explores GTD step four, Reflect. Many have spoken of this fourth step in GTD as being confusing. The confusion reduces when you consider that 'Reflect' isn't a passive activity. It isn't just about heading off to a quiet place to think deeply about all that is and could be. No, 'Reflect' is a very tactical part of the system. It is used at different times for different reasons. GTD brings a lot of attention to weekly activities around reviewing commitments and the progress being made. GTD also makes mention of the decision process we go through every other moment of the week when we face choices about what to do next or if to stop something. Whilst necessary, most find it difficult to keep these reviews going. Their enthusiasm wains. As with all habits, establishing them is aided by having more than one reason. Raising awareness of core values and what is important to you helps in this regard.

COACHING CORNER: Mastery in accountability.

To achieve mastery in accountability you need to be doing the following:

Step 1: Use your lists.

It sounds kind of obvious, but often, when you find yourself frustrated with lack of progress or having a feeling of under-achieving, it is because you have not used your lists of decisions. Instead, you have just gone and done what is on your mind. All the effort put into presence, awareness and crafting is totally in vain if you don't use the outcomes of those activities. To use the lists, you read them at any point where your next activity isn't set by a time commitment (i.e., a calendar diary entry). Instead of just doing what you have in your head, which if skill one is being used, should be nothing, you must read the lists. The loud 'do this now' voice in your head may be guiding you to the most important thing at any moment, but it is also possible that it is not. As we explored in chapter thirteen and the workings of the mind using the theatre metaphor, that thing that is loud in your mind, might be on stage simply because you haven't externalised it properly.

The hard truth is that you will never have enough time in your life, no matter where you are in the journey, to do everything you should, could, need, or want to do. The list of things to do will always be longer than the amount of time you have. The key is to have an efficient process to get to the bottom of what is the most important thing to be doing at any given moment, so that you can be certain that your time is being used properly. Once you have this efficient process in use, you will reach choice without burden. This means you will be doing the most important thing to be doing at that moment and hold no guilt or regret about what you are not doing.

Using your lists ensures that you are choosing the most important thing to be doing at any given moment.

Step 2: Be realistic

To achieve the benefits of choosing the right thing to be doing at any given moment: firstly, you need to finish the thinking about things you want to do (i.e., awareness). Then you need to organize the results of that thinking (i.e., crafting). And finally, you need to make time to use this thinking to make decisions about what you will do at any given moment. That decision process involves three parts. Firstly, you need to consider the context you find yourself (i.e., trying to do actions that require an internet connection when you are at 35,000 feet in economy is only going to wreck your head). Secondly, you need to look at how much time you have before the next time-based commitment (i.e., there is no point starting something that takes sixty minutes if you only have thirty before the next meeting). Finally, you need to consider your resources, your energy, and attention (i.e., there is no point starting something that requires good concentration when you have just come out of a mentally draining conversation).

When you consider context, time available and energy, you are better placed to know very quickly which of the things on your lists, is the most important thing to be doing at that moment.

Step 3: Clean as you go.

Completing actions is crucial to achieving your goals; however, losing track of where you are with respect to all associated actions will slow you down. It is important, therefore, that when you finish one action, you close the loop and update your lists with the next action. This housekeeping activity is part of the skill of crafting; however, it is the skill of accountability that will ensure you update the lists and therefore don't forget.

Periodically, perhaps weekly, you must clean up your list of actions. When you get busy, you might take short cuts. Your list of things to do can become less than effective. There are usually two things that typically cause you to avoid using your lists of decisions. Firstly, you have written down a 'task' to save time, when you should take a few moments more to qualify what is the actual next physical thing that will move this forward. These 'tasks' don't get done, because your mind goes into overdrive every time you read them. The second reason your lists need cleaning up is because the level of importance has changed (i.e., while it was important when you wrote the item on the list, it is no longer as important as other things you decided you will do).

Periodically, perhaps weekly, you must look over the list of commitments you have made to yourself, to others, and those which others have made to you. These commitments should be maintained in a list of projects, and delegated lists, as outlined above under mastery in crafting. Reviewing these lists ensures that you have a good sense of the bigger picture. As the week progresses, you might find you have completed an action or two and forgot to add the next action onto your lists. Reviewing the list of aims on your projects list, provides the opportunity to catch things that may be about to fall between the gaps (i.e., to avoid missing a commitment to someone else). This regular review also provides the space to remind yourself of commitments that have been made by others and gives you the opportunity to follow-up again.

You must also do regular housekeeping on your filing (i.e., monthly or quarterly). In supporting the commitments that you make, you will accumulate stuff. This stuff includes physical things, emails, social media updates, news, other forms of instant messaging and, of course, thoughts. All these things are stored somewhere, even if just temporarily while you use them. If you don't regularly purge these places, they get too full and cumbersome and once that happens, you won't use them, or you will just pile more stuff on top.

Accountability is by far the hardest skill to master. With the motivation that comes from understanding who you are, mastery is easier but still not guaranteed. The problem relates to habits and the way the chemicals in our brains react to what we are doing. Chris Bailey presents these challenges in an easy to grasp and entertaining way. In summary, brain fuel, as explored in chapter sixteen, in addition to being used for thinking and organizing, it is used to do things that are enjoyable and fun. As a result, it is hard for us to change ourselves to be doing the things we know are better for us, when there are plenty of just as enjoyable activities beckoning for our attention.

The key to mastery in accountability is accepting that you are human, that willpower isn't enough, and to use external triggers and accountability levers to build the habits you need. We will explore this further in chapter twenty-one.

Mastery in focus

Mastery in focus is crucial to achieving anything close to agency. It is the essential skill in seizing the moment. Focus is the thing that allows you to experience your potential. It is crucial in creating the wonderful things you are capable of sharing with the world.

Mastery in focus is demonstrated in your ability to stay on task for the time it requires, be it minutes, or hours. That takes energy. Using energy effectively requires knowledge. To do that you need a deep understanding of what you are good at (i.e., your traits). Things that you are good at raise your energy, while other things deplete it.

Mastery in focus is also about reducing distraction and training your mind to do that. In his writing on productivity, David Allen, addresses the concept of mastery in focus within GTD step five, Engage. This is the step where the rubber hits the road. Furthermore, in his book, Chris Bailey emphasizes the need to exercise the attention muscle and how it helps reduce the impact of distraction.

And finally, Mastery in focus is about creating the conditions that enable it. Cal Newport writes extensively around this idea. In his work, *Deep Work: Rules for Focused Success in a Distracted World*, Newport includes countless examples of how we can utilize both shallow and deep focus to drive our productivity. Newport also shares the evidence about how we miss the opportunity to develop thinking skills, by not managing our distractions effectively and efficiently. Knowing your limitations helps you create habits and conditions that allow you to focus.

David Allen's *Mind Like Water* is another lovely piece on mastery in focus and everything to do with the art of agency. Allen talks about the idea of a stone hitting a calm pond. When the stone hits the water, the pond absorbs the stone. There might be a splash or waves, or just ripples, however eventually the water returns to calm. It is as if the stone never dropped into it. Allen suggests that in performing at our best, we must bring ourselves to have a mind like the calm pond, so that with each new input, interruption, or distraction, we are able to handle it efficiently and effectively with ease. Then return, as soon as possible, to a calm pond-like state.

Mastery in focus is crucial to being on the path of your own choosing. It is through this focus that you understand the true nature of your experiences.

Chapter 21: The Art

How often have you heard others, and perhaps yourself, claim to be living for the moment. Maybe that claim is supported with phrases like 'I have no regrets' or 'life starts now.' Have you considered what any of that really means, or how to achieve it?

The rocking chair

Imagine you are in your twilight years enjoying the moment sitting in your rocking chair on your veranda, looking back over your life. Imagine you are reflecting and seeing no point where you regretted a decision or something you did. Here is the problem with that. Most can barely remember the details of a few months ago, never mind the whole of their life up until this point. When you are in your twilight years, are you really going to remember every moment and every decision and be certain that you didn't make a bad choice, or that you did something that you now regret. The best that you can hope for is to have the confidence that when you reflect, you know that at every point you made the best decision you could, given where you were, the environment around you, and the knowledge you had at the time.

The challenge is that unless you apply yourself, it's unrealistic to think that you will be making the best decision in any given moment. Unfortunately, the busy mind struggles to see everything that you want or need. It even struggles to see everything in your immediate view and the consequences of action or inaction. Without this full awareness you will struggle to make effective decisions.

Most would like to think that they are on top of everything they need, want or should do, and all the commitments they have. The reality is that most are only aware of a fraction of those things. Furthermore, that is only a starting place. It takes real focus to really appreciate the impact of your decisions and how to make them in a way that aligns with what is true for you in the context of where you are aiming.

It can be comforting, for a time at least, to hide in our past achievements and choices. When you succumb to the busyness or when you fail to adjust your goals based on new perspective, you lack agency.

Meaning

When you explore what is important to you, do you ever get drawn to 'happiness' or 'joy'? Have you ever considered what that means?

If happiness was what truly motivated you, then you'd just be drunk or high all day long. Staying loaded would solve the 'happiness' problem so long as you never sober up. For most, what drives us is something different.

Meaning, or fulfilment in life doesn't come from happiness and joy. It is derived from responsibility. From taking responsibility for yourself, for those around you, for your community, and for your society at large. It is the adventure or the process of taking responsibility which gives us fulfilment and meaning. That is because fulfilment isn't an endpoint. It is a process.

As an example, take the concept of looking after yourself physically, like working out at the gym, but also sleep and nutrition. You can have others cook for you. You can take pills for sleep. You can even take pills and so forth to replace exercise or have your body modified to repair the damage resulting from the lack of care. These actions will get you the outcome, without you participating in the experience of getting there. However, this can leave you feeling less than accomplished. The reward or outcome is not proportionate to the effort you put in.

The adventure of taking responsibility is in the act of looking after yourself and others, in the right manner, to achieve the outcome or realise the reward. The responsibility you take might induce difficulties, challenges, sweat, and tears, but it also generates engagement and reward. That is the adventure. And that is where meaning and fulfilment is found.

Dwelling

You will likely have fond memories of times in the past, perhaps with family and friends. Times of laughter and joy. There is comfort in reflecting on good times. It helps lift yourself back up after a fall. However, too much dwelling is a distraction. It takes you away from interacting and engaging with the new situation. Too much time spent re-living the past joys reduces the time that can be put toward facing the realities of the present. It reduces your focus and awareness. Furthermore, being overly fond of the past creates an unhealthy connection to how things should be in the present. A tendency to want the present routines to match the past can take you away from fully experiencing what the present moment has to offer.

The risk associated with dwelling on past joys, applies also to dwelling on past pain, or the pain that resulted from your choices. As already discussed, sitting back in your rocking chair and claiming that you have no regrets is not realistic. Nor is it useful to chastise yourself over past failings. You can't fully know the consequences of all your choices, ahead of making them. Some consequences will cause pain for yourself or others. Reflecting does have a significant benefit; in that it allows you to find better ways to experience the world. However, dwelling on what you didn't get or do, or the bad outcomes that resulted from your actions, risks you only seeing things through a negative lens. That can limit your options. You may sell yourself short and go after things that aren't going to utilize your full potential or meet your needs.

Mindset

Your state of mind is crucial to how you reflect on and use your choices. It impacts the set of options you see. If there is ever a cloud over your state of mind as you move into unchartered territory, it is useful to take stock of where you have come from, what you have, and fundamentally, be grateful for it all.

COACHING CORNER: *Taking stock.*

The process to take stock is as follows:

First, look back, asking these questions and writing a list for each:
- 'What am I grateful for?'
- 'What do I have?'
- 'What were the high points in the past period?'

It doesn't matter so much if there is overlap across these lists, just make sure five to ten minutes is given to each question. Once the lists are done, reflect on the answers to these two questions:
- 'What do I want?'
- 'What action am I willing to take right now in order to move forward?'

These questions are designed to help surface actions that are constructive, aligned to what's important to you, and are in context of where you are now.

Life is such a wonderful collection of experiences. Some experiences beckon you to engage with them. Agency is aided by focusing on those experiences that beckon you to engage with them. When you do engage, you must allow those experiences to change you. It is through the change that you move forward.

While it is helpful for you to enjoy memories or get excited about something in the future, you mustn't dwell in either place. Dwelling on what has or might happen, reduces your ability to see the present and the options it provides. Similarly, dwelling on a specific future, limits the options you see. Too much focus on the past or the future, has you at risk of missing an opportunity in the present that may take you forward quicker or more effectively.

Not being overly focused on the past or the future is not the same as meandering through each moment, just waiting for the end. Agency requires vigilance and being awake to the possibilities of each experience.

The growth opportunity

Perfecting the art of using experiences to forge your path involves two challenges. First, you must move beyond the busyness. You must move to a place where you can think with a clear mind and be ready for anything. Then you must let go of the past, get beyond limiting beliefs, and engage in what is immediately before you.

COACHING CORNER: Engaging in the moment.

To engage fully in the moment and leverage the experience to help you change and grow, you can ask yourself specific questions at any given choice. Some examples of the specific questions are:

- 'What does this mean to me?'

- 'What does this feel like?'
- 'What does this tell me about me?'

It is through these focused questions that the true nature of the experience becomes evident. That enables you to see the learning opportunity. In this place you have less resistance to replacing the beliefs that served you up until that moment.

Maintaining momentum

Maintaining momentum is important if you have any hope of making the necessary adjustments at the right frequency to avoid the challenge proposed earlier with respect to the rocking chair.

A well tried and tested method for maintaining momentum is the daily use of active questions as proposed by Marshall Goldsmith and Mark Reiter, in their 2015 book, *Triggers, Creating Behavior that Lasts, Becoming the Person You Want to Be*. This involves establishing Active Questions in your daily routine.

These self-reflective-based questions start with, 'Did I do my best to' and end in something that you are working towards. Examples would include, 'to be a committed team member', 'to be a caring friend', 'to be a loving spouse, and 'to be an engaging parent'.

COACHING CORNER: Active questions.

The process to experience active questions is as follows:

1. Take a piece of paper and write down the aims or behaviours you are hoping to adopt or adjust (i.e., exercise regularly).

2. Now, think of how you would measure your progress by considering what question could assess if you are doing what

you committed to (i.e., 'Did I go to the gym?'). Write those 'measurement' questions on a separate page. Repeat this for each of the items on your aims and behaviours list.

3. Next, for each of the 'measurement' questions, ask yourself how you performed in the context of yesterday (i.e., 'Did I go to the gym?'). If this is a new behaviour, ask as if you have already started. Give yourself a score between zero (0) and ten (10), where zero is farthest from where you want to be and ten is closest. Write the scores next to the measures. As you ask the questions, observe what you start thinking about. When done, turn over the page or hide the 'measurement' questions and their scores.

4. Now, on a further piece of paper, write a new set of 'measurement' questions, but this time start them with 'Did I do my best to' (i.e., 'Did I do my best to go to the gym?')

5. Finally, for each new 'measurement' question in the 'Did I do my best' format, reflect on yesterday again. Once more, give yourself a score between zero (0) and ten (10), where zero is nowhere near your best and ten is your absolute best. Write the scores next to the measures. As you ask the questions, observe what you start thinking about.

After doing this exercise you will likely find that active questions are less critical of your performance. This is because you immediately have context of what was happening yesterday. And, more importantly, the active question has your mind looking for proactive ways to move forward. Often, we fall short of what we want to achieve because we fail to use measures that drive us forward instead of holding us back. Normal measures are too focused on what you knew at the time of defining the measure and don't consider the context of where you have found yourself later. Changes in context include things that change in your surrounds that are beyond your control (i.e., weather, serious illness, death as well as changes in your home life, workplace, and communities).

The best practice is to construct a set of active questions and then score them on a regular basis, perhaps daily. Over time the questions change, as your context, and needs shift.

Below are some examples of active questions to use daily:

- Did I do my best to balance my intake of food with my use of energy?
- Did I do my best to grow and learn?
- Did I do my best to capture my aims and statements of gratitude?
- Did I do my best to be an authentic father?
- Did I do my best to experience companionship?
- Did I do my best to experience intimacy?
- Did I do my best to be an authentic son?
- Did I do my best to be an authentic brother?
- Did I do my best to be an authentic friend?
- Did I do my best to maintain the conditions for being my best - personally?
- Did I do my best to maintain the conditions for being my best - professionally?
- Did I do my best to create the conditions for Otherish Giving?
- Did I do my best to write?

COACHING CORNER: *Scaling Questions.*

A good method for identifying what you can do about any aspect where you are falling short of what you desire, is the use of the Scaling Question process.

This process helps clarify the current position or relationship to a question, and then induces a positive mindset in bringing focus to the actionable next steps.

Step 1 - Pick an area or topic that you want to look at.

Step 2 - Score it, 1-10

Think about the topic, give it a score between 1 and 10, where 1 is the furthest from where you want to be and 10 is the closest.

Step 3 - Reflect on the score

Considering the score given above, ask yourself 'What makes this a [n] not a [n ÷ 2]'

For example, if you gave an aspect a score of 4, you would ask yourself, 'What makes this a 4 not a 2'.

Reflect on this question for a moment or two. Allow the mind to answer the question.

Write down what your mind comes up with, perhaps start a bullet-point list. Ask the question again after writing your first answer. Then ask it again and try to get a third reason. It is ideal to get two to three reasons. Avoid allowing your mind to take the next step just yet. You don't need to think about what would make it higher or why it is at this score. Just focus on the question.

Step 4 - Look forward at options

Next, ask yourself 'What would it take to bring this score to a $[n+2]$'. For example, if you gave a score of 4, you would ask yourself, 'What would it take to bring this score to a 6?'.

Once more, allow your mind to reflect on the question for a moment or two.

Try to find specific actions that you can take right now. Ask the question once or twice more to give yourself more possible options.

Step 5 - Take action

Finally, ask yourself 'What will I commit to doing?'

This process can be used in conjunction with the results of daily active questions to help you keep moving forward positively.

The Ego

In managing your path and journey, there is one final hurdle. This is possibly the hardest to avoid and yet the most important. While you may consult externally when making decisions, ultimately, it is with yourself that you must agree. Without that internal agreement, you will have no chance of being on the path of your choosing. You will lack agency.

When you are challenged or feeling strongly about a course of action or inaction, you must listen to your self-talk. The thinking that comes from these voices in your head will have two influences. The first is aligned with ego and the other is aligned with your true purpose (i.e., agency).

Ego is steering you when you feel yourself responding in an aggressive or defensive manner to a change in conditions or an unexpected event. The ego-driven self-talk will look for ways to change something about that new condition or unexpected event. If that something is good and is happening directly to others, the ego will look to take the rewards or diminish the value of that good thing. If that something is bad and happening directly to others, the ego will relish that it isn't happening to you, try to get away from it before that bad thing comes your way or act the hero and intervene before truly understanding the relevance of that something. If the something is good and is happening to you directly, the ego will either feel guilty and undeserving of such a good thing or show off, claiming it for itself, and ensuring everything was because of the ego's action, when that might not be the case. If the something is bad and it is happening to you directly, the ego seeks to blame someone or something else. The ego will put distance between you and any related action that might have led to that change in conditions or unexpected event. Worse still is that the ego is possibly not aligned with your path. It will likely be aligned with what you perceive others find important.

The alternative is agency. Firstly, and foremost, agency influenced self-talk doesn't differentiate between 'happening to me' or 'happening to you'. It understands that something is simply happening. Secondly, when having agency, you feel there is opportunity and learning, no matter if the something is good or bad. Alignment with agency ensures the something is integrated into your path. When the something is good, agency will ensure the experience is rich and engaging, and that there is maximum opportunity for growing and maintaining momentum. When the something is bad, agency will look for the meaning in the experience to learn from it, but also to find ways to minimize its impact so it is less painful or upsetting for all involved.

COACHING CORNER: *Managing the ego.*

The trick to managing the ego is to listen to your self-talk. Listen for the conditional statements. Listen for thoughts that involve changing someone or something. Equally, listen for self-talk relating to blaming someone or something for things not being a certain way. And finally, be aware when your thinking is trying to justify something based on someone else's beliefs. Look for it in others too. They may think they are helping you, but it might be their ego talking, not agency. Here are some examples of the self-talk you may hear when the ego is influencing:

'To achieve this, she should …'
'This would have worked if only he had …'
'She needs to do … before I can do …'
'I can do that better than they can; I should intervene'
'I can't do that because of …'
'That can't happen until …'
'I can't be that until … happens'
'I am so much better than this, if only I …'
'That will never happen without first …'
'This always happens when I …'
'We must do it this way because … says so'
'I can't do it that way because it says so in …'

When you sense this type of conversation, look for unconditional facts. Engage in those fact-based thoughts and that encourages agency. Here are some examples:
'It's cold.'
'It's hot.'
'I am frustrated.'
'I am fearful.'
'I am tired.'

'I am hungry.'
'The sun is warm.'
'I am excited.'
'I am healthy.'
'I am loved.'
'He is professional.'
'They are a great team.'
'She has the company's interests at heart.'
'We have an excellent product.'
'We have wonderful children.'
'We want the best for each other.'
'We want the best for our children.'

Allow the thoughts that come from those statements to spread through you and replace any self-talk about changing something or someone. A focus on truths should help you see the actions available to you in the current context. You should see what can be done right now, given the resources at your disposal, your talents, and considering the constraints of your circumstances at that precise moment. Agency will drive you closer to your true aims when the ego isn't getting in the way.

Take aim

In striving to take a path of your own choosing, you must manage the ego. Otherwise, it will overwhelm you, and eventually take over completely. While it is important to give these ideas consideration, taking the ego seriously isn't. Eckhart Tolle suggests we should play with it. Tolle suggest we should humour the ego and make fun of the suggestions it gives us. Through that play we achieve agency.

When you entered the world, everything was new and wonderful. You had no resistance (i.e., there was no fear, disgust, boredom, hate, envy, sorrow, anger, frustration, discontentment, alarm, or indifference). You were authentic. The ego didn't have a role yet. However, you were helpless. You didn't understand how to engage in the context you'd been flung into. For most of us, we are nurtured into the world safely. We are conditioned and given notions of what's good or bad, or dangerous, or safe. That builds resistance around things that would potentially harm us or cause discomfort. This is where Ego comes in.

As a teenager you protected yourself with largely resistance driven behaviours. The Ego would have driven how you engaged and moved forward. It allowed you to only exist based on other's perspective on what is good, bad, right, or wrong. While is serves its purpose then, if left unchecked that ego and related resistance holds you back.

As you grow more aware of your values and traits, dismantle limiting beliefs, and master presence, awareness, crafting, accountability, and focus, you break through the resistance that nurtures the ego. You live in the present. The BS fades away. You claim your purpose. You have mastered the art of agency.

Reference

- Allen, David; *Getting Things Done. The Art of Stress-free Productivity* (2015 ed)
- Bailey, Chris; *The Productivity Project: Accomplishing More by Managing Your Time, Attention, and Energy* (2016)
- Brann, Amy; *Neuroscience for Coaches* (2015)
- Collins, Jim; *Good to Great: Why Some Companies Make the Leap... And Others Don't* (2001)
- Crawford, Shelley; *Resilience Building Model* - https://www.linkedin.com/in/shelley-crawford/
- Downey, Myles; *Effective Coaching, Lessons from the Coach's Coach* (2003).
- Drucker, Peter; *The Effective Executive* (1967)
- Gallwey, Timothy; *The Inner Game of Tennis* (1974)
- Goldsmith, Marshall, and Reiter, Mark; *Triggers: Creating Behavior That Lasts--Becoming the Person You Want to Be* (2015)
- Goleman, Daniel; *Emotional Intelligence: Why It Can Matter More Than IQ* (1996)
- Goleman, Daniel; *The Brain and Emotional Intelligence: New Insights* (2011)
- Goulston, Mark. Ullmen, John; *Real Influence: Persuade Without Pushing and Gain Without Giving In* (2012)
- Goulston, Mark; *Just Listen: Discover the Secret to Getting Through to Absolutely Anyone.* (2009)
- Goulston, Mark; *Talking to 'Crazy': How to Deal with the Irrational and Impossible People in Your Life* (2015)
- Grant, Adam; *Give and Take: Why Helping Others Drives Our Success* (2014)
- Kegan, Robert. Laskow Lahey, Lisa, *Immunity to Change: How to Overcome It and Unlock the Potential in Yourself and Your Organization* (2009)

- Kisin, Konstantin, An Immigrant's Love Letter to the West (2022)
- Kofman, Fred. *Conscious Business: How to Build Value Through Values* (2006)
- Kundera , Milan, The Unbearable Lightness of Being (1984).
- McKeown, Greg; *Essentialism. The Disciplined Pursuit of Less.* (2014)
- Newport, Cal; *Deep Work: Rules for Focused Success in a Distracted World* (2016)
- Peterson, Jordan B; *12 Rules for Life. An Antidote to Chaos* (2018)
- Peterson, Jordan B; *Beyond Order, 12 more rules for life* (2020)
- Pink, Daniel H.; *To Sell Is Human; The Surprising Truth About Moving Others* (2012)
- Arendt, Hannah; Eichmann in Jerusalem: A Report on the Banality of Evil (1963)
- Rock, David; *Your Brain at Work: Strategies for Overcoming Distraction, Regaining Focus, and Working Smarter All Day Long.* (2009; revised 2020)
- Salovey and Mayer; *Emotional Intelligence* (1990).
- Sanders, Tim; *Love Is the Killer App: How to Win Business and Influence Friends* (2002).
- Seligman ME1, Steen TA, Park N, Peterson C; *Positive psychology progress - empirical validation of interventions* (2005)
- Sheldon & Lyubomirsky; *How to increase and sustain positive emotions - The effects of expressing gratitude and visualizing best possible selves* (2006)
- Thompson, Neil, and Thompson, Sue; *The Critically Reflective Practitioner.* (2008)
- Tolle, Eckhart; *The Power of Now: A Guide to Spiritual Enlightenment* (2001)
- Walker, Matthew; Why We Sleep: The New Science of Sleep and Dreams (2017)
- Whitecloud, William; *The Last Shaman* (2012)

Index